Letts
gets you through

KS2 ENGLISH
SATs SUCCESS
REVISION GUIDE

Ages 7–11

KS2 ENGLISH SATs

REVISION GUIDE

SHELLEY WELSH

Contents

Reading

Fiction Writing

Non-fiction Writing

Grammar and Punctuation

Spelling

Speaking and Listening

SATs Practice Questions

Choosing the right book

Do you enjoy reading? Is it something you do for pleasure or do you see it as a school task – or even a burden? Think about the different texts you read: books, websites, texts, emails, newspapers, magazines, comics – even the back of a cereal packet in the morning as you eat your breakfast!

Do you prefer **fiction** or **non-fiction**? Horror or fantasy? Books about animals or humans? Don't just pick a popular book because your friends do – make your own mind up. Read what interests you!

Once you know what type or **genre** of book you prefer, how do you know which book will interest you? Read the **blurb**. Never buy or borrow a book without checking out the blurb on the back. It's a brief summary of the plot (sometimes called a **synopsis** or **précis**).

You may know the expression 'don't judge a book by its cover' but you often **can** judge a book by its cover. Also, don't feel that a book which contains illustrations is just for younger children.

Top tip!

In fiction writing, the narrator and the author may not be the same person. Often the narrator is a character in the story, speaking from their point of view, not the author's.

Keywords

Fiction ➤ Made-up stories
Non-fiction ➤ Factual information
Genre ➤ Type or kind of writing
Blurb ➤ A brief summary of the book on the back cover
Synopsis / précis ➤ Brief summary
Empathise ➤ To understand and share the feelings of someone else

Fiction

Stories made up by the author are **fiction**. They may be based on truth, such as stories set in World War II.

A good story should hook you in from the start and make you want to read on. Usually the author will want us to **empathise** with the main character or characters; 'empathise' means understanding the feelings of someone else. If we don't like the main character or characters, we might not care enough to read on.

How many fiction genres can you think of?

play scripts, thrillers, fairy-tales, myths and legends, stories from other cultures, historical

adventure, romance, fantasy, horror, sci-fi, mystery, poetry, traditional tales

Non-fiction

Non-fiction writing can be information and facts about a range of subjects.

Information and explanation books tend to have the same features, which are:

- contents page
- index
- glossary
- illustrations, pictures, tables, graphs and diagrams.

Explanations include *how* and *why* something happens. How many other non-fiction genres can you think of?

newspaper articles, adverts, autobiographies, biographies, persuasive writing

information, explanation, recounts and non-chronological reports

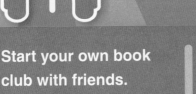

 **Have a go!** Start your own book club with friends. Decide how long you need to read a book, taking it in turn to choose, then meet to discuss. Did you like the book or not, and why?

 **Test yourself**

❶ What is the purpose of the blurb on the back of a book?

❷ Write a definition for:
a. fiction
b. non-fiction.

❸ What do you do if you are 'empathising' with someone?

❹ What does 'genre' mean?

Imagery and figurative language

Imagery is a writer's use of vivid and descriptive language to help the reader visualise what is being described in a text. This language is known as **figurative language**. Figurative language is often used in poetry.

A description might also be **multi-sensory**, which means it will appeal to more than one sense: see, hear, feel, taste and smell.

You may be asked to discuss and evaluate how authors use figurative language and the impact it has on the reader. Three forms of figurative language are:

similes   **metaphors**   **personification**

Similes

When a writer finds similar characteristics in two things and compares them, it is known as a **simile**. The words 'like' or 'as' are used in similes.

The princess lay quite still, her skin **as** pale **as** a pearl.

With a heavy heart, Seb walked to school, **like** a slow old snail.

After her long illness, Chloe felt **as** fragile **as** a spider's web.

Metaphors

Metaphors are also a comparison between two things but, unlike similes, the words 'like' and 'as' are not used. In a metaphor, the writer is saying the object **is** the thing they are comparing it to.

My tears were rivers flooding down my cheeks.

My best friend, **Ajamil**, **is a walking dictionary**.

Top tip!

Look for the words **like** and **as** in descriptive writing to help you identify similes.

Personification

Writers use **personification** when they want to give human characteristics to a non-human thing.

> The children cautiously entered the yawning cave, which soon consumed them.

The writer has said that the cave is 'yawning' to show it has a wide opening like a human's mouth. 'Consumed' makes it seem as if the cave has eaten the children.

> The gnarled and twisted fleshless fingers of the hunched trees brushed the forest floor in the wind.

> Giant waves ranted and raged at the little boat, licking it furiously with foamy white tongues.

Keywords

Imagery ➤ The use of figurative language to help the reader visualise what is being described

Figurative language ➤ The descriptive language used to create imagery

Simile ➤ A comparison of two things with similar characteristics

Metaphor ➤ When the writer says the object that is being compared actually *is* the thing it's compared to

Personification ➤ Giving human characteristics to a non-human thing

 **Have a go!** Build up a bank of figurative language as you read so that you can use it in your own descriptive writing.

 **Test yourself** **Listen up 2**

1. What is personification?
2. What are the underlined words being compared to in the following sentences?
   a. The girl sang as sweetly as a nightingale.
   b. The seas were a surging swell of boiling liquid.
   c. We lay beneath a sun of burning lava.
   d. The goalkeeper was as cool as a cucumber.

Three more forms of figurative language are:

onomatopoeia   **alliteration**   **assonance**

Onomatopoeia

Onomatopoeia is the use of words that sound like the thing they are describing.

BOOM!   SPLAT!   MEOW

You might use onomatopoeia to indicate a loud or gentle sound in your descriptive writing.

onomatopoeia

SPLAT! The knight shoved the fire-breathing dragon hard against the castle wall.

High in the rainforest's canopy, Azmir could hear the soft rustle, rustle of the whispering leaves.

onomatopoeia

onomatopoeia

The repetition of the word 'rustle' also serves to show that the sound was continuous.

Alliteration

Alliteration is repeating the initial sounds of words close to each other. In your descriptive writing, use alliteration sparingly otherwise it might come across like a nursery rhyme! You will often see examples of alliteration in poetry.

The turtles were **s**wept across the **s**oft **s**and toward the **s**ea.

'Whereat, with **b**lade, with **b**loody **b**lameful **b**lade,
He **b**ravely **b**reach'd his **b**oiling **b**loody **b**reast.'

Assonance

Assonance is the repetition of vowel sounds inside words, sometimes called internal rhyme. Again, you will often come across it in poetry. You might have heard the following line in a song in the film 'My Fair Lady'.

> The r**ai**n in Sp**ai**n falls m**ai**nly on the pl**ai**n.

Here are some other examples:

> The scavenging cr**o**ws flew l**o**w over sn**o**w-capped mountains.

> And I liked the b**ea**st on the **ea**st b**ea**ch l**ea**st.

Keywords

Onomatopoeia ➤ Words that sound like the thing they are describing

Alliteration ➤ Repetition of the initial letters of words next to or close to each other

Assonance ➤ Repetition of vowel sounds inside words

Parent tip!

Don't worry, your child won't be expected to be able to spell onomatopoeia, as long as she/he can say it, use it and identify it.

Top tip!

Use figurative language when discussing poems. Some poems might have examples of all the different types of figurative language, whereas some will just have one or two.

Have a go!

Create a bank of onomatopoeic words for you to dip into when doing descriptive writing.

Test yourself

❶ Underline the assonance in these sentences:

   a. My fine time in Hawaii soon went by.

   b. Creeping up past my knees, the sea was three feet deep.

❷ Circle the alliteration and underline the onomatopoeia in these sentences:

   a. 'Pop!' went Pippa's pink party balloon.

   b. The gentle splish-splash of the surging sea sent me to sleep.

Over the next six pages you will find texts that have been annotated with the answers to questions which test your **comprehension** (understanding).

When you have read a text that you are being asked questions about, you might want to **skim read** the passage again, to reinforce your understanding of it. Then, when you are answering the questions, you will need to **scan** the text to find the words, phrases and clauses that link to the questions.

The simplest types of questions ask you to find information in the text. Other questions ask you to 'read between the lines' or **infer** characters' feelings, thoughts and motives from their actions, and justify these inferences with evidence from the text. Some questions will ask you to predict what might happen from details that are stated or implied in the text.

Read the texts below and on the opposite page, then answer the questions, referring to the annotations to see if you are correct.

Q2 This simile shows the reader that Lucy was still feeling the effect of being on the ship because the ground seemed to be going up and down like a ship on the waves.

Q1 The ship is described as being 'like a great bright insect'.

Extract from *The Voyage of the Dawn Treader* by C.S. Lewis

Lucy was of course barefoot, having kicked off her shoes while swimming, but that is no hardship if one is going to walk on downy turf. It was delightful to be ashore again and to smell the earth and grass, even if at first the ground seemed to be pitching up and down like a ship, as it usually does for a while if one has been at sea. It was much warmer here than it had been on board and Lucy found the sand pleasant to her feet as they crossed it. There was a lark singing.

They struck inland and up a fairly steep, though low, hill. At the top of course they looked back, and there was the *Dawn Treader* shining like a great bright insect and crawling slowly northwestward with her oars. Then they went over the ridge and could see her no longer.

Q3 'Delightful' tells us that Lucy is happy (this paragraph is written from her point of view so this is what she is thinking).

Q4 A ship. The clues are: Lucy had come 'ashore', so most likely she had come from a ship; the *Dawn Treader* was heading 'northwestward with her oars', which tells us more definitely that it is a ship. Also, the phrase 'it had been on board' is a further clue.

① What simile is used to describe the ship?

② Why is the simile 'like a ship' used to describe the ground?

③ Which adjective tells us that Lucy is feeling happy?

④ What is the *Dawn Treader*?

   a. a giant sea snake   **b.** a ship   **c.** an aeroplane   **d.** a giant insect

Q1 'into the descent' means the climber has started to climb down the mountain.

Q2 Kuni was on 'exposed ground' that had previously avalanched and she wanted to get down.

Extract from *Mortal Chaos* by Matt Dickinson

Kuni was into the descent, moving as fast as she could down the steep ice field when her radio went off in her pocket.

'Kuni, this is base camp. Base camp, over.'

Her first reaction was to ignore it, she was on extremely exposed ground and she knew that the slope had avalanched in the past with catastrophic results. Worse still, she could see a narrow crack had opened up in the face, a grey shadow of fractured ice which snaked almost fifty metres across the summit pyramid. Kuni knew it was a potentially lethal sign, that the snowpack had shifted, a clear cut indication that the face was definitely not stable.

But the radio blurted out again and through the rising wind Kuni thought she heard the words 'your father'. She came to a halt, pushing her ice axe deep into the snow to act as a support, then took the radio out of her pocket.

'This is Kuni.'

'We've got your father on the line! Wait just a moment.'

Q3 The expanded noun phrase 'potentially lethal sign' tells us Kuni's life could be in danger.

Q4 Kuni is clearly very brave. The evidence for this is that she was on a slope that she knew had avalanched in the past with catastrophic results. Despite this, she stopped to answer the radio.

1. What does the phrase 'into the descent' mean?

2. Why did Kuni ignore her radio call to start with?

3. Find an expanded noun phrase that tells the reader Kuni's life could be in danger.

4. What do you infer about the type of person Kuni is from the text?

Keywords

Comprehension ➤ Understanding

Skim read ➤ A quick reading technique to help you get the gist (main idea) of a text

Scan ➤ A quick reading technique to help you find specific words, phrases and clauses in a text

Infer ➤ To form an opinion about something based on the information given rather than from an explicit statement

Test yourself

1. **Answer this question about *The Voyage of the Dawn Treader*.**
   Why does the narrator say that it was 'no hardship'
   for Lucy to be barefoot?

2. **Now answer these questions about *Mortal Chaos*.**
   a. Why is 'snaked' an effective way of describing the crack in the face?
   b. Which clause tells the reader that Kuni stopped?

Listen up 4

Reading poems

Read the poem through and try to feel the rhythm. Does it rhyme? Don't panic if it doesn't make sense at first! Then skim through it, stopping at the end of each verse to consider the meaning. Finally, when answering the questions, scan through the text to find the answers.

Read the poem extracts on these two pages, then answer the questions, referring to the annotations to see if you are correct.

Q1 The moon is described as being 'a ghostly galleon tossed upon cloudy seas'. The road is described as a 'ribbon of moonlight over the purple moor'.

Q2 The moon was out which tells us it was night time. Also, words like 'darkness' and 'jewelled sky' tell us it was night. The inn being 'locked and barred' implies it is night time as during the day an inn would be open.

Q3 The hard **c** sounds in 'cobbles he clattered and clashed' make you think of the clack of the horse's hooves on the hard cobbles. 'Tapped' is also onomatopoeic as it sounds like the rap made by the highwayman's whip.

Q4 The repetition gives the line rhythm; it emphasises the continuous movement of the horse.

First three verses of *The Highwayman* by Alfred Noyes

The wind was a torrent of darkness among the gusty trees.
The moon was a ghostly galleon tossed upon cloudy seas.
The road was a ribbon of moonlight over the purple moor,
And the highwayman came
    riding—Riding—riding—
The highwayman came riding, up to the old inn-door.

He'd a French cocked-hat on his forehead, a bunch of lace at his chin,
A coat of the claret velvet, and breeches of brown doe-skin.
They fitted with never a wrinkle. His boots were up to the thigh.
And he rode with a jewelled twinkle,
    His pistol butts a-twinkle,
His rapier hilt a-twinkle, under the jewelled sky.

Over the cobbles he clattered and clashed in the dark inn-yard.
He tapped with his whip on the shutters, but all was locked and barred.
He whistled a tune to the window, and who should be waiting there
But the landlord's black-eyed daughter,
    Bess, the landlord's daughter,
Plaiting a dark red love-knot into her long black hair.

1. What metaphors are used to describe the moon and the road in the first verse?

2. How do we know that the events occur at night? Use evidence from the poem to support your answer.

3. Find one example of onomatopoeia in the third verse.

4. What is the effect of repeating the word 'riding'?

Rain in Summer by
Henry Wadsworth Longfellow

Q1 The rain is 'beautiful' because it is a welcome relief 'after the dust and heat' and will cool the temperature down.

How beautiful is the rain!
After the dust and heat,
In the broad and fiery street,
In the narrow lane,
How beautiful is the rain!
How it clatters along the roofs,
Like the tramp of hoofs! ←

Q2 The simile he uses is: 'like the tramp of hoofs!'

How it gushes and struggles out ←
From the throat of the overflowing spout!←
Across the window pane
It pours and pours;
And swift and wide,
With a muddy tide,
Like a river down the gutter it roars ←
The rain, the welcome rain!

Q4 The effect of the repetition emphasises how much rain there is and how relentlessly it pours down.

Q3 You might choose the phrase 'struggles out' as people or animals normally struggle, not rain. Alternatively, 'from the throat of the overflowing spout' gives the spout a human feature – a throat. Finally, the use of the word 'roars' gives the rain a human sound, making it seem like a living, roaring being.

1. Why do you think the poet says rain is 'beautiful'?

2. What simile does the poet use in the first verse to describe the sound of the rain?

3. Find an example of personification in the second verse.

4. What is the effect of repeating the word 'pours'?

Test yourself

1. **Answer these questions about The Highwayman.**

   a. **What does the phrase 'jewelled sky' in verse two tell you?**

   b. **Why do you think the poet repeats the word 'riding' in the first verse?**

2. **Now answer these questions about Rain in Summer.**

   a. **What does the phrase 'muddy tide' tell us about the rain?**

   b. **What simile does the poet use in the second verse?**

Listen up 5

Reading plays

Plays are written in a different format from novels. They are meant to be performed rather than read but are still great to read. At the beginning of a play script, we are usually told some background information about the main characters and their relationships. The characters tell us the story through dialogue, though some plays might have a narrator as well to provide more detail. Stage directions (usually in brackets) tell you where actors and props should be, what is going on around them and the manner in which they should say something.

Read the short play below, then answer the questions, referring to the annotations to see if you are correct.

What an Excuse!

Time:	Present day
Place:	Dad and Monika are talking to each other in the kitchen.

MONIKA: Great tea Dad, thanks. I'm off to play games on my tablet now.

DAD: Hold on young lady! You haven't done your chores yet!

MONIKA: Aww, come on, chores? What chores?

DAD: Well, for starters, you need to help me with the washing up. (*Pointing to the dirty dishes*)

MONIKA: (*Shakes head*) Oh no Dad, I can't do that. All that soapy water will ruin my nails!

DAD: Riiight! Well OK then, you can take the rubbish out. (*Hands rubbish bag to Monika*)

MONIKA: (*Shakes head again*) Outside? I can't do that. It's dark outside and all scary! My friend Vikram took the rubbish out in the dark the other night, and slipped on a slug! What happens if I do that?

DAD: Do you mean six-feet-tall Vikram, the rugby player? Hmm… (*Dad looks unconvinced*) You weren't scared of the dark last night when you were playing with your friends in the field! And it's very unlikely you are going to slip on a slug! OK then, please go and vacuum your room and make your bed. (*Opens cupboard under the stairs and points to vacuum*)

> Q2 Vikram is a tall, rugby player and it seems funny that a big, strong person like that would slip on a small creature such as a slug.

> Q3 Dad doesn't quite believe Monika's story about Vikram.

MONIKA: Oh no Dad, I can't do that. Think of all the dust up there – you know I have a dust allergy – I'll spend the rest of the night sneezing!

DAD: Yes, that is true. But the dust won't stop you tidying up, will it?

MONIKA: I can't possibly do that Dad. I saw the hugest, biggest spider on one of my books the other day. I can't tidy up until I am sure it has gone. (*Gives a small shudder*)

DAD: You and your 'spider phobia'! (*Dad bends the forefingers on both hands to indicate inverted commas*)

MONIKA: But we could make some cupcakes? Baking is sort of like a chore, isn't it?

DAD: Nice try! But no, that isn't a chore. And I don't have time to bake because I will be doing all your chores!

MONIKA: Oh … Well… I guess drying the dishes won't totally wreck my nails, and actually I quite like the dark. Perhaps that spider has gone outside. So maybe I could do my chores.

DAD: Great idea! And after you have finished, we can make those cupcakes! (*They smile at each other*)

Q4 Dad doesn't really think it's a spider phobia but more of an exaggeration on Monika's part, so he shows her this by putting the spoken phrase in inverted commas, just as one would the written phrase.

Q5 Monika realises that the baking won't happen if Dad does her chores so she might as well do them herself.

1. How would you describe Monika's dad's personality?

2. Why is Monika's story of what happened to Vikram humorous?

3. What does the author mean by 'dad looks unconvinced'?

4. Explain why Monika's dad indicates inverted commas around his phrase 'spider phobia'.

5. Why does Monika change her mind and agree to do her chores?

Q1 You could choose from: **patient**, **firm but fair**, **persistent**, **sarcastic** or similar.

Listen up 6

Test yourself

1. What is the purpose of stage directions in a play script?

2. What are the missing words in the sentence below?

The story of a play is told through .... and sometimes a ....

3. What do you think the stage direction 'Exit stage right' after a character's lines means?

4. From reading the play extract *What an Excuse!*, what sort of girl do you think Monika is?

Information texts

Information texts inform the reader about a subject. They are usually set out with a title, sub-headings to organise information into sections and pictures with **captions** or **annotated** (labelled) diagrams. Vocabulary is usually technical and the writing is formal. Most books include a contents page, an index and a glossary. Websites are a good source of information, with links to related information. You need to be able to summarise the main ideas in the text and identify the key details that support them.

Look at this web page below about the mountain lion then answer the questions, referring to the annotations to see if you are correct.

The Mountain Lion

The mountain lion is a large cat found throughout most of South and North America. Other names for this cat include puma, panther, cougar and red tiger.

Mountain Lion, mammal
Habitat: mountain, grassland, forest, desert
Diet: carnivore
Life span: 9–11 years

Mountain lions eat mainly deer (in North America) but also smaller creatures such as rabbits and mice. They cache their prey under leaves and soil, so they can come back to it over the course of a few days.

Despite having a poor sense of smell they have excellent hearing and vision, which helps them to hunt early in the morning and in the evening. They stalk their prey until it is close enough, and then they pounce. They have very powerful hind legs which allow them to jump very large distances – up to 12–13 metres (40–45 feet).

Cubs are born with spots and blue eyes. However, their spots have usually disappeared by the time they are nine months old and their eyes change to yellow by the time they are 16 months old. The young cats are normally independent by 18 months when they leave their mother to fend for themselves.

Q1 Two features that help the mountain lion hunt.

Q2 'cache' is a synonym for 'hide' and 'stalk' is a synonym for 'pursue'.

Q3 It means the young cubs have to look after themselves because they leave their mother.

❶ Find two features of the mountain lion that help it to hunt.

❷ Find a synonym for the word 'hide' and the word 'pursue'.

❸ What does the phrase 'fend for themselves' mean?

Keywords

Caption ➤ Brief description of what is shown in a picture

Annotated ➤ Labelled

Explanation texts

Explanation texts provide the reader with information about the subject they are covering, at the same time explaining **how** or **why** something happens. Explanation texts also tend to include annotated diagrams, charts or pictures (with captions) to help you understand. Vocabulary is technical and the writing is formal.

Read this short extract about hurricanes and answer the questions, referring to the annotations.

Q1 The metaphor of 'birth' describes how a hurricane is created.

Q2 A wind pattern near the ocean surface enables air to spiral inward.

How are Hurricanes Created?

The birth of a hurricane requires at least three conditions. Firstly, the ocean waters must be warm enough at the surface in order that enough heat and moisture are absorbed into the overlying atmosphere. This is what provides the potential 'fuel' for the hurricane. Secondly, moisture from sea water evaporation has to combine with that heat and energy to provide the power needed to propel a hurricane. Thirdly, there has to be a wind pattern near the ocean surface to spiral air inward. Then thunderstorms form, allowing the air to warm further and rise higher into the atmosphere. As long as the winds at these higher levels are fairly light, this structure can remain intact and grow stronger: the beginnings of a hurricane!

Q3 The thunderstorms allow the air to warm further and rise higher into the atmosphere.

Q4 The author's exclamation makes it seem like he is in awe of hurricanes.

1 What metaphor does the writer use to describe the creation of a hurricane?

2 What enables the air to 'spiral inward'?

3 Explain the impact of the thunderstorms on the air.

4 Why do you think the writer ends his final sentence with an exclamation mark?

Test yourself

1 What six features would you expect to find in both information and explanation texts?

Adverts

Adverts use bold, eye-catching images and large, colourful fonts to persuade you to buy their products. They might use **rhetorical questions** – questions used for effect, where no answer is expected.

Sometimes they use celebrities to attract your attention and to make you think: "If it's good enough for them, it's good enough for me!" or even: "Maybe I will be more like them if I use this!"

Often there is a special offer or deal to encourage you even further. A catchy **slogan**, or a **jingle** if it's a TV or radio advert, will plant itself in your memory so that every time you hear it, you think of the product.

Look at this advert then answer the questions below, referring to the annotations to see if your answers are correct.

Q1 Bold product name and picture of famous footballer.

Q2 They are healthy, they are hand-picked, they are eaten by a famous footballer and there is a special offer.

Q3 Alliteration; exaggeration ('the best', 'can't get any healthier'), celebrity support, special offer, rhetorical question ('Can you afford NOT to buy them?')

The best baked beans!

BONZ BAKED BEANS

Beans can't get any healthier!

- hand-picked beans
- no preservatives
- 5 varieties

If they're good enough for **Fabio Fabloos**, they're good enough for *YOU!*

Special offer – Buy One, Get One Free
Can you afford NOT to buy them?

❶ What are the two main things that grab your attention in the advert?

❷ What should make you want to buy this product?

❸ Which persuasive techniques are used in the advert?

Persuasive writing

Persuasive texts also use a range of techniques, such as **rhetorical questions** and **emotive language**, to persuade the reader to agree with the writer's point of view.

Read this persuasive text then answer the questions, referring to the annotations.

Should Children Use Mobiles?

For many people, a mobile phone is the latest must-have fashion item. Children are no exception; some as young as six years old have the most up-to-date, hi-tech phones and are merrily texting, emailing and playing on-line games to their heart's content. However, is society on a slippery slope now that mobile phones have become 'the norm'?

Certainly, many busy parents encourage this diversion from family interaction. It's the easy option: rather than entertain your children, give them a mobile phone and you'll have peace and quiet. What happened to board games and chatting round the kitchen table? Both are things of the past for far too many families these days.

> **Q2** 'a slippery slope' means that society could be going 'downhill' as so many people now use mobile phones.

> **Q3** Busy parents will have peace and quiet and not have to entertain their children.

> **Q1** Copy this rhetorical question.

1. Find and copy the rhetorical question that shows the author is concerned about family life.
2. Which expanded noun phrase in the first paragraph means that with so many people using mobiles, society could be at risk?
3. Why does the writer think giving children a mobile phone is the 'easy option' for busy parents?

Keywords

Rhetorical question ➤ A question used for effect and with no answer expected
Slogan ➤ A short, memorable phrase in an advert
Jingle ➤ A short verse or tune designed to be memorable
Emotive language ➤ Emotional language used to express feelings

1. Answer these questions on the text 'Should Children Use Mobiles?'
   a. What does the phrase 'the norm' mean?
   b. What two examples of 'family interaction' does the writer give?

Balanced argument

A balanced argument gives both points of view, though sometimes you can detect if the writer is **biased**, or supports one point of view over another.

Read this argument below, then answer the questions, referring to the annotations to see if you are correct.

Should Pupils Have to Wear School Uniforms?

As children move up through the education system, they naturally become more independent, inquisitive and want to know 'WHY...?' about a lot of things. One of these is why they have to wear school uniform. Have children got the right to say 'NO!' to wearing it?

Some people believe that wearing a uniform helps children stay focused on their studies; rather than chatting about the latest fashion that everyone is wearing, they can get on with their learning. On the other hand, many children believe that they learn best when they are wearing their own, individual-style clothes, rather than a stiff and uncomfortable school uniform.

Having a school uniform means that parents on low incomes aren't pressurised into having to buy their children the latest designer clothes and, likewise, their children aren't feeling as if they are the 'odd one out'. However, school uniform is not cheap! Some schools insist that the uniform is bought from one particular shop, thus meaning parents are unable to shop around.

Q2 Children's learning might be affected if they are all sitting around talking about the latest fashion that everyone is wearing.

Q3 Parents on low incomes might feel they had to buy their children the latest designer clothes.

Q4 You might get a bargain or cheaper selection if you could shop around.

1. Do you think the writer of this text is biased or unbiased in their views? Support your answer using evidence from the text.
2. How does the writer suggest that wearing their own clothes might affect a child's learning?
3. What pressures might parents on low-incomes face if there was no school uniform?
4. What could be an advantage if school uniform was available in more than one shop?

Q1 The writer is unbiased because he gives reasons for both wearing and not wearing uniform. The writer says having uniforms means parents on low incomes don't feel they have to buy designer clothes but, on the other hand, uniforms often cost a lot because there is only one shop that sells them.

Keyword

Bias ➤ Supporting one point of view over another

Listen up
9

Test yourself

1. In 'Should Pupils Have to Wear School Uniforms?' why might some children feel they are 'the odd one out'?

Fact and opinion

It is important to know the difference between **fact** and **opinion** when reading and writing non-fiction. You might have an opinion about a television programme you have watched or a book you have read; this is how you **personally** feel about something.

Facts are not what you think or feel – they are true pieces of information. When a journalist is writing a newspaper article, they are supposed to report the facts of a story, not their opinion, allowing you to make up your own mind.

In this report, the writer gives both opinions and facts.

fact – Jessica is a writer

fact – where Jessica lives

opinion

opinion

opinion

fact

opinion

"Streets Getting Worse"

Jessica writes about crime on the streets near her.

"In London the streets are getting worse. Around Bermondsey where I live, people walk around the streets and see when you're on your own. They see what people have on. They choose what they will have off you, like jewellery. You can't wear it nowadays, you don't know what will happen to it, so watch out.

They ask for your phone. One of the ways this can happen is they'll ask you for the time – then ask about your phone. It also happens at schools. Some schools have had to have assemblies to tell children to hide their phones or not to bring them to school. I know what it feels like, so be careful on the streets."

Top tip! Try to get in the habit of reading a newspaper and discussing interesting articles with a family member or friend. *First News* is often found in school libraries and contains a wide range of child-friendly articles.

Facts

This report about William Shakespeare just gives the facts; the writer doesn't give an opinion, so we don't even know if they **like** Shakespeare's plays! It's not relevant.

Who was William Shakespeare?

Shakespeare was born in Stratford-upon-Avon, Warwickshire, in 1564. Very little is known about his life, but by 1592 he was in London working as an actor and a dramatist. Between about 1590 and 1613, Shakespeare wrote at least 37 plays and collaborated on several more. Many of these plays were very successful both at court and in the public playhouses. In 1613, Shakespeare retired from the theatre and returned to Stratford-upon-Avon. He died and was buried there in 1616.

What did he write?

Shakespeare wrote plays and poems. His plays were comedies, histories and tragedies. His 17 comedies include 'A Midsummer Night's Dream' and 'The Merry Wives of Windsor'. Among his ten history plays are 'Henry V' and 'Richard III'. The most famous among his ten tragedies are 'Hamlet', 'Othello', and 'King Lear'. Shakespeare's best-known poems are 'The Sonnets', first published in 1609.

Top tip! Sometimes an opinion can be expressed as if it were a fact, e.g. The friendliest dogs are Labradors (where 'I think …' is left out).

Listen up 10

Keywords

Fact ➤ A piece of information that is true

Opinion ➤ What you personally think about something

Test yourself

❶ **Decide whether the following sentences are fact or opinion.**

a. **Dogs are friendly, loyal pets.**

b. **It usually snows in the Alps in winter.**

c. **The Earth orbits the Sun whilst it spins on its axis.**

d. **The best show on the TV is *The Simpsons*.**

Newspaper articles

Newspaper articles tell us about something that has happened. The headline should grab your attention; often **puns** (word play) are used to make them humorous.

GREAT-GRANDMOTHER'S GREAT TRAIN ROBBERY!

72-YEAR-OLD lady holds up train station with a banana!

Shelley Cardigan looks like your normal, beloved elderly relative. She has snow-white hair tied up in a bun and glasses. She loves knitting and looking after her two great-grandchildren. She looks totally harmless, but Shelley is currently serving a prison sentence for robbery!

Four months ago, Shelley (from Blackpool in Lancashire) robbed a train station. She put a stocking over her head, pretended she had a gun under her coat (actually a banana) and boldly walked into her local train station. She threatened the ticket officer and demanded £100. Shelley, always so well-mannered, smiled, said, 'Thank you' and left. However, she was caught by police soon after.

Shelley told our reporter, 'I was widowed two years ago and I was just craving a bit of excitement. Now I'm famous. I've been on TV and in the newspapers.' When asked if she would do it again she smiled and said sweetly, 'I think once is enough don't you?'

> **Q3** You don't normally expect great-grandmothers to be robbers. Also there is alliteration in **G**reat-**g**randmother's **g**reat…

> **Q4** The adverb 'boldly' tells us that she was confident about what she was doing.

> **Q2** Shelley was desperate for some excitement in her life.

> **Q1** Choose six from the text, e.g. **1.** her name is Shelley Cardigan; **2.** she is 72 years old; **3.** she lives in Blackpool; **4.** she robbed a train station; **5.** she is in prison; **6.** she has two great-grandchildren.

1 Find six facts about the robber in the newspaper article.

2 What was Shelley's reason for stealing money from the train station?

3 How does the headline catch your attention?

4 What does the adverb 'boldly' tell you about how Shelley approached her crime?

Keyword

Pun ➤ A type of word play where a word can have more than one meaning

FIRE AHEAD! *by James White*

LAST night, police and the fire service were called to an incident at a sports complex on the outskirts of Shrewsbury. A fire had broken out in the main building while children were taking part in an archery contest on the floodlit playing field.

The archery field

Three young men in black hoodies and jeans were seen fleeing the premises at the Bollington Leisure Complex, confirming suspicions that the fire was not an accident. Two men were caught and taken away for questioning, while the third is still on the run.

Lucy Dalton, aged 11 and a member of the Archery Kids Club, said, 'One minute we were firing arrows at our target boards, the next we heard "FIRE!" It was all terribly confusing.'

Jon Courtney, manager of the complex, told our reporter at the scene: 'Our security has been stepped up dramatically in recent months, following a spate of crimes in the local area.'

One eyewitness, a parent, said that it was a real blow that the children were forced to stop halfway through such a nail-biting archery competition when they had practised so hard and for so long.

Q1 They were seen running away from the sports complex.

Q2 The competitors were firing arrows and when Lucy heard "FIRE!" she might have thought it meant that she should fire her arrow, not that it was a warning that there was an actual fire.

Q3 One parent said it was a 'nail-biting' competition, which means you are on the edge of your seat / excited.

1. Why are the three young men suspected of starting the fire?
2. Why did Lucy think it was confusing when she heard "FIRE!"?
3. What adjective indicates that the competition was exciting?

Test yourself

1. In 'Great-grandmother's Great Train Robbery!' what was funny about Mrs Cardigan saying 'thank you' to the ticket officer?
2. In 'Fire Ahead!' how do we know that the manager takes security at the complex seriously? Use evidence from the text to support your answer.
3. In 'Fire Ahead!' what was particularly disappointing for the children about having to stop the competition?

This mind map will help you remember all the main points from this topic. Have a go at drawing your own mind map.

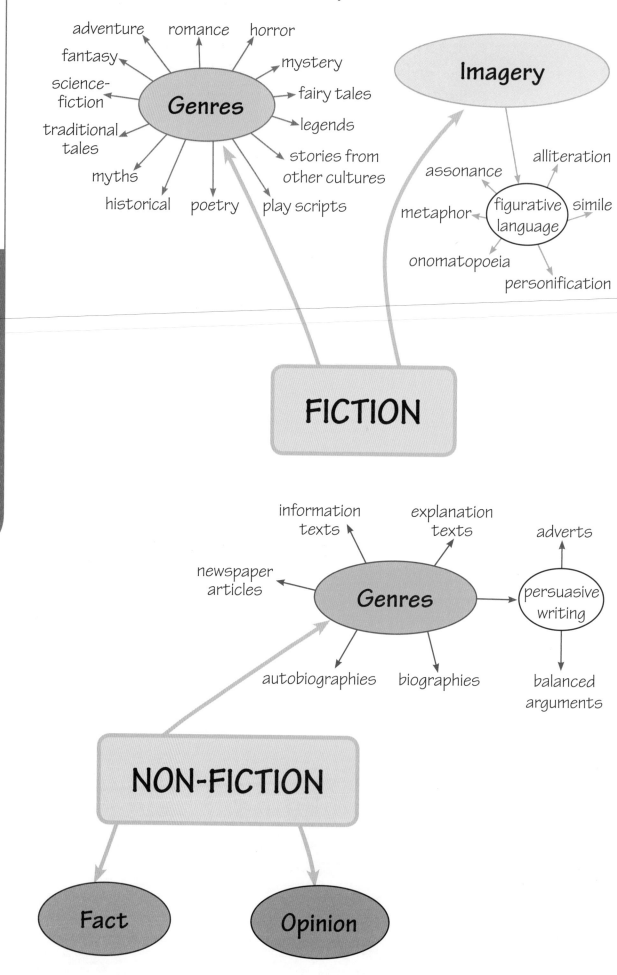

adventure romance horror

fantasy

science-fiction

traditional tales

myths

historical poetry play scripts

Genres

mystery

fairy tales

legends

stories from other cultures

Imagery

assonance

metaphor

onomatopoeia

figurative language

alliteration

simile

personification

FICTION

information texts

newspaper articles

explanation texts

adverts

Genres

persuasive writing

autobiographies biographies

balanced arguments

NON-FICTION

Fact

Opinion

1 Highlight examples of personification used in the following verse. **(2 marks)**

> Rain splinters town.
>
> Lizard cars cruise by;
> Their radiators grin.
> Thin headlights stare –
> shop doorways keep
> their mouths shut.

2 Where do we find information about the position of props and characters for a staged play? **(1 mark)**

....

3 Write suitable **similes** for the following:

a. My little sister is as chatty as .... **(1 mark)**

b. The wind howled like .... **(1 mark)**

c. The branches hung low like .... **(1 mark)**

d. My hair stood on end like .... **(1 mark)**

4 In the table below, tick whether the text genres are fiction or non-fiction. **(4 marks)**

	Fiction	Non-fiction
sci-fi story		
autobiography		
explanation		
poem		

5 Circle the facts and underline the opinions in the following text: **(11 marks)**

Dear Sir/Madam

I rarely complain about anything but after the shocking meal I had when I was in your restaurant last night, I feel compelled to put pen to paper.

The pasta was barely warm and extremely soggy. This is an easy product to cook so it's not difficult to get it right. The waiter, in a sulk about something, brought our drinks after a very long wait. I was on the verge of drinking the water from the vase of flowers in front of me. In this day and age, when unemployment is at an all-time high, I would have thought he would want to do his best!

Audience

Always consider your audience before you start writing. A reader wants to be entertained and you can do this by using a range of vivid vocabulary, interesting sentence structures and an exciting – but simple – plot. Don't have too many characters, too much dialogue or a complicated plot; they will slow the story down.

Read the extracts below. Which one do you, as a reader, prefer?

1 I walked down to the river bank. I sat down in the sun.

2 Lazily, I ambled down to the mossy river bank where I gratefully flopped down to bask in the sun's warm rays.

The second extract uses adverbs, adjectives and interesting verbs, which give the reader a more vivid mental image of the scene.

1 We went into the forest. Then we hid. We were scared of the beast.

2 Tiptoeing cautiously to avoid detection by the blood-thirsty beast, we hid beneath the twisted, gnarled arms of the trees that had been bent double by the raging storm.

This time it's not only adverbs, adjectives and verbs in the second extract that enhance the sentence but also the use of personification: the 'gnarled arms of the trees' gives the trees human characteristics.

Planning

Time spent planning is time well spent. How you plan is a very personal matter – some people like to do bullet points; others might use a mind map. If you have been given a prompt, keep referring to it so that you stay on task.

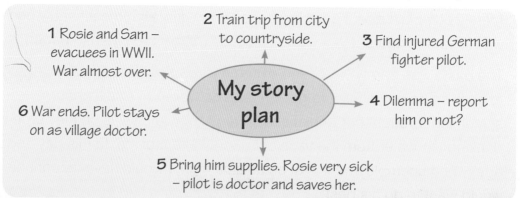

1 Rosie and Sam – evacuees in WWII. War almost over.

2 Train trip from city to countryside.

3 Find injured German fighter pilot.

My story plan

4 Dilemma – report him or not?

5 Bring him supplies. Rosie very sick – pilot is doctor and saves her.

6 War ends. Pilot stays on as village doctor.

Writing

Now that you have your plan, you can start to write. Say each sentence in your head before you write it, thinking of how you can make it better.

What are your personal targets? They could be any or all of the following examples:

- vary sentence starters
- use accurate punctuation
- use a wider range of vocabulary
- use interesting adverbs, adjectives and verbs
- use figurative language.

Shall I write, 'The dog barked at the children' or 'The vicious dog barked aggressively at the petrified children'?

Proofreading

Check your work as you go and **proofread** it at the end. This means checking:

- spelling, punctuation and grammar
- how interesting your sentence starters and vocabulary are
- **cohesion**.

If your writing has cohesion, it means the whole piece fits together clearly, and sentences and paragraphs link together.

Listen up 12

Keywords

Proofreading ➤ Checking your writing for errors and ways to improve it
Cohesion ➤ When your whole piece of writing fits together clearly so that it makes sense

Top tip! Self-edit as you write, as well as at the end when you proofread. If you've finished but wish you'd used a metaphor somewhere, put a * above where you would like it to go and write it at the end. It's never too late!

Have a go! What would you say are your main writing targets? Remember five or six that you could keep in your head for when you write.

Test yourself

❶ Proofread the following passage, improving the language used as well as the punctuation, grammar and spelling.

As we went towards the cliff edge, we ~~soon~~ saw a boat with big sales going across the horizon from the bow in the bad whether someone waved at us to come aboard.

Fiction Writing

Story openings

There are many ways to start a story. When you were younger, you will have read a lot of stories that started with 'Once upon a time there lived a…' The opening of a story is very important because it's the **hook** that draws the reader in and makes them want to keep reading!

Look at these different openings:

Question: Can you keep a secret?

Dialogue: "Where's Father going with my goat?" Maria asked her mother as they were setting the table for dinner.

Middle of action: The howling wind attacked my face as I clung desperately to the sheer cliff face, not daring to look below.

Characters

Weave the physical appearance and personality traits of your main character or characters into your writing as you go, rather than doing it just once at the start of your story. Use how they look to reflect aspects of their personality. If it's a striking part of a character's appearance, then you could weave it in at a relevant point. For example:

As Erin and Stella made their way through the dense, tree-tangled forest, Stella tripped, snagging her long blonde hair on a thorn bush. "Help me!" she cried, pools of liquid starting to form in her deep sapphire eyes…

Listen up 13

Keyword

Hook ➤ In this context, it's what grabs the reader's attention

Characters (continued)

In this description from Lemony Snicket's *A Series of Unfortunate Events*, Klaus's glasses and wide range of reading material support the narrator's view that he is intelligent.

> Klaus Baudelaire, the middle child, and the only boy, liked to examine creatures in tidepools. Klaus was a little older than twelve and wore glasses, which made him look intelligent. He was intelligent. The Baudelaire parents had an enormous library in their mansion, a room filled with thousands of books on nearly every subject. Being only twelve, Klaus of course had not read all of the books in the Baudelaire library, but he had read a great many of them and had retained a lot of the information from his readings.

Top tip! Weave in character and setting descriptions throughout your whole story.

Settings and atmosphere

Think about the atmosphere you want to create in the setting – is it a happy place to reflect the mood of the characters and the plot, or is it dark and grim, reflecting some danger your characters find themselves in?

Look at the setting description in this extract from *The Graveyard Book* by Neil Gaiman:

> Bod stopped beside a grave that looked the way he felt; it was beneath an oak that had once been struck by lightning, and now was just a black trunk, like a sharp talon coming out of the hill; the grave itself was water-stained and cracked, and above it was a memorial stone on which a headless angel hung, its robes looking like a huge and ugly tree-fungus.

A sinister mood or atmosphere is created by the graveyard setting and the blackened tree trunk, which is compared to a 'sharp talon'. The personification of the memorial stone as a 'headless angel' further gives the audience a shiver down the spine! Which was the author's intention of course…

Have a go! Choose a family member or friend to describe. What sort of observations would you make about their personality and their appearance? What adjectives best describe them?

Test yourself ❶ What different ways could you start a story opening?

Fiction Writing

There are lots of different types of poem. These are just a few:

- list
- performance
- concrete
- acrostic

- haiku
- limerick
- calligram

Using kennings to write a poem

A **kenning** is a two-word phrase or compound word that describes an object without actually giving its name. For example, 'mouse-catcher' to describe a cat.

What animal might these kennings be talking about?

Tree-stomper
Bush-eater
Pond-splasher
Trunk-waver
Tusk-thruster

Read this poem: 'Brilliant Dad'.

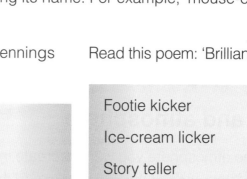

Footie kicker

Ice-cream licker

Story teller

Genuine fella

Cake baker

Feel-safe maker

Never sad

Brilliant dad

Haiku

A traditional Japanese **haiku** is a three-line poem with five syllables in the first line, seven in the second line and five in the third line.

Haiku poems are usually about nature.

Springing to new life
Flowers dance in the cool breeze
Searching for warm sun.

Limericks

Limericks are funny, five-line poems which always start with: There was… The first two lines and the last line rhyme; the third and fourth lines rhyme.

There was an Old Man with a beard,
Who said, 'It is just as I feared!
Two Owls and a Hen,
Four Larks and a Wren,
Have all built their nests in my beard!'

Listen up
14

Concrete poem

A **concrete** poem is sometimes called a shape poem. It is where the poem is written in the shape of the main subject of the poem.

Star!
Shining bright
in the black velvet night.
A jewelled and twinkling comfort light.
A high golden diamond
Shining bright.
Star!

Have a go!

Write a poem about a bird using kennings. Here are two compound words to help you:

full-throttle; sky-diver.

Test yourself

1 What are the features of a haiku?

2 How many lines does a limerick have?

3 What is meant by a 'concrete poem'?

Fiction Writing

This mind map will help you remember all the main points from this topic. Have a go at drawing your own mind map.

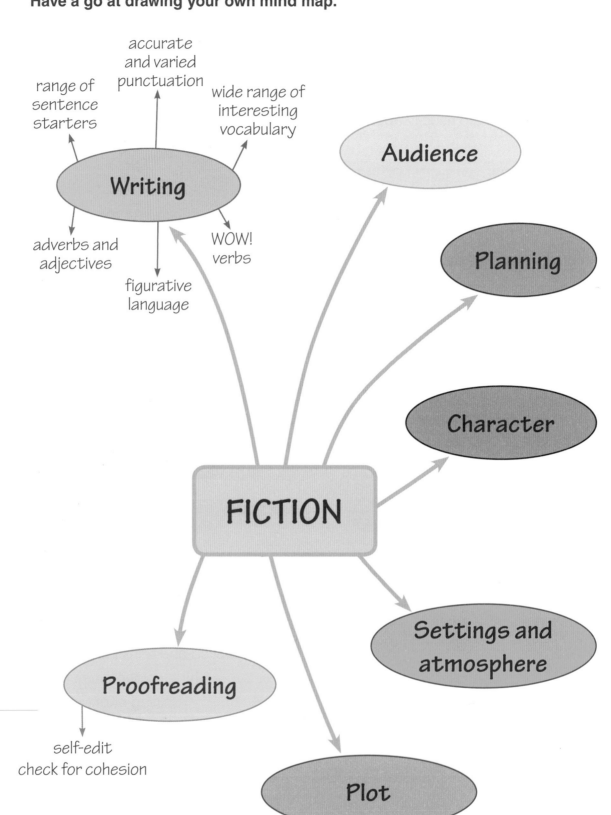

accurate and varied punctuation

range of sentence starters

wide range of interesting vocabulary

Writing

adverbs and adjectives

WOW! verbs

figurative language

Audience

Planning

Character

FICTION

Settings and atmosphere

Proofreading

self-edit
check for cohesion

Plot

1. Write a paragraph for points 3 and 4 in this story plan, describing the dilemma Miles and Becky face when they are forced to take shelter in the cave.

You can write in the third person or in the first person from either Miles's or Becky's point of view. Continue on a separate piece of paper if you need more room. **(5 marks)**

2 Setting:
On the beach

3 Dilemma:
Tide comes in very fast.

1 Main characters:
Miles and Becky.

My story plan

6 Ending: Coastguard gives them hot chocolate to warm them up.

4 Next setting:
Take shelter in a cave.

5 Resolution: They find a tunnel which takes them up to the top of a cliff.

....

....

....

....

....

....

2. Write either a haiku or a concrete poem about a subject of your choice in the box below. **(5 marks)**

Writing an information text

Before writing, always familiarise yourself with the genre by reading examples. Information texts might come in leaflet form (easy to get in your local library, museums, travel agents or even in your school reception area), books, posters or websites.

Can you find evidence of the following features?

- Bold title to inform reader of subject
- Subheadings to organise information into sections
- Bold and coloured fonts and underlining, so key words stand out
- Bullet points
- Pictures or diagrams

Information books may also include a contents page, an index and a glossary.

Give the reader information about what you are writing about. What are the most important and interesting facts? How can you present these so they stand out to the reader?

Main title →

Who were the Vikings?

The Vikings came from Denmark, Norway and Sweden (Scandinavia). The name Viking means **pirate raid**, a word from the **Old Norse** language. The Viking period was approximately AD 700 to 1100. Many Vikings left Scandinavia and travelled to countries such as Britain and Ireland where they fought, stole treasure or settled as farmers, craftsmen or traders.

Subheading for organising information into sections. →

<u>Viking ships</u>

Viking ships were designed to be fast to make battles and raids easier. They were called **dragon ships** or **long ships**. They used slower boats for carrying cargo and passengers called **knorrs**. For fishing or short trips they used smaller boats.

Key words in bold.

Explanation texts

Explanation texts have similar features to information texts but include an explanation of how or why something happens. The title might be in the form of a question such as 'How does the Earth spin on its axis?' or 'Why do some animals sleep through the winter?'

Paragraphs are often introduced by subheadings. Words and phrases such as 'because', 'for this reason' and 'consequently' might be used to explain the 'how' or the 'why'.

Title written as a question to tell reader what is being explained.

Key words in bold.

Why do plants disperse their seeds?

Seeds need to grow away from the parent plant, otherwise the young seedlings will be competing with one another and their parent plant for water, **nutrients** and sunlight. For this reason, seeds move away from the parent plant in order to have the best possible chance of growth and survival. Plants use different methods to spread their seeds. Some **species** depend on the wind, others on water. Some depend on animals, including humans.

Explains why they need to grow away.

Explains that there are different methods of spreading their seeds.

Explains how the seeds are spread.

Top tip! When planning a piece of information or explanation writing, choose three to five sub-headings and jot down some notes about what you will cover in each section. You can leave a space or a blank box for where an image might go, but remember, you won't get marked on artwork, just your writing!

Have a go! Think of a subject you find really interesting. How would you present it as an information leaflet or flier to get someone interested? Fold a piece of A3 paper into three even sections so that it looks like a leaflet, then get to work! Otherwise, use Publisher in Microsoft Office.

Test yourself

1 What are the main features of an information text?

Adverts

Adverts use a range of persuasive techniques to convince you to buy a product. Text is kept to a minimum and is big and bold. Images should be eye-catching and act as a hook to get your attention. There may be a special offer or a **rhetorical question**. Sometimes **command verbs** are used (verbs that tell you to do something) and repetition. There might be a **slogan** (a short, memorable phrase that makes you think of the product).

Adverts are **biased**, which means they are one-sided – they are only telling us the good things about a product. TV and radio adverts use music and jingles to make you remember the product every time you hear it!

Positive words like **healthier**, **fitter**, **more successful**, **happier**, **exclusive**, **free**, **radiant**, **shinier** are used, depending on the product being advertised. Some adverts use a celebrity to help convince you to buy the product. This tactic will work really well if you admire the celebrity!

product name in bold with use of alliteration

YUM-YUM YOGHURT
"I've never felt so young and healthy or looked so fit and radiant!"

rhetorical question

exaggeration

celebrity to promote the product

Do you want to feel like Chloe?
Buy Yum-Yum Yoghurt today.
Feel the difference instantly!
In all major supermarkets NOW!

special offer

**Promotional offer:
Buy 2, get 1 free**

*Lazing on sandy shores...
listening to the gentle lap
of the waves...*

No stress, no noise, no pressure.

Who wouldn't want a holiday like this?

repetition

rhetorical question

Only 3 km from the picturesque beach is the medieval village of Eze, nestled high in the cliff tops with the most stunning view of the crystal-clear Mediterranean. Restaurants in this area are out-of-this-world: eat like kings, safe in the knowledge that prices are sensible.

exaggeration

Persuasive writing

We use persuasive writing to convince someone that our point of view on a subject is right or their point of view is wrong. Make sure you stick to the subject, argue your point in a reasonable way and don't attack the reader personally. It's fine to use **emotive language** (express your emotions) but don't be rude.

Persuasive writing uses the following features:

- emotive language
- flattery
- statistics to back up your point
- rhetorical questions
- repetition
- exaggeration

> Dear Mr Brown
>
> I am writing in response to your notice in last week's local paper that planning permission has been granted for the construction of a leisure centre in the woodland on the outskirts of town. I know that you have a very important job and you are extremely busy ← **flattery** but I do hope I can persuade you to move the centre to the other side of the motorway.
>
> Our woodland is a precious part of the community, used regularly by old and young alike. Eighty-five per cent of people asked in a recent survey confirm this. ← **statistics to back up your point** Can you really justify destroying this beloved area of natural beauty? ← **rhetorical question** It's shocking to think you would even consider such sabotage! ← **exaggeration**

emotive language

Keyword

Command verb ➤ A verb used to give a command

Listen up 16

Have a go! Design an advert for a new hair product. For example: gel, mousse, spray.

Test yourself ❶ Name six features of persuasive writing.

Non-chronological reports

You might need to write a **non-chronological** report in History, Geography or Science, not just in English lessons. This is a type of information text.

The first step in writing a non-chronological report is to read up on the subject you are writing about. Then plan what you will write about in your report – a mind map or bullet points can help you organise ideas. Try to split your subject up into subheadings; these will be your ready-made paragraphs!

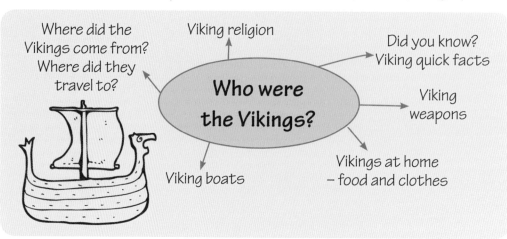

You might want to include an annotated diagram to support your information. However, don't spend too long on 'artwork' – the writing is a lot more important.

Once you have chosen a title, think about your opening sentence or sentences. This should tell the reader what you are writing about.

> Vikings were sea-faring Scandinavian warriors in early medieval times. They had a reputation for being fierce raiders, plundering other lands before settling there.

You can then start to write about the main sections of your report under subheadings.

Top tip!

Learn the features of non-chronological reports; they have the same features as information texts:

- title
- introduction
- subheadings to introduce sections / key features
- summary
- technical vocabulary and formal writing
- fact, not opinion.

Listen up 17

Recounts

Recounts are retelling something that has **happened**. They are written in the past tense.

They might be an account of a visit, an account of an event in history, a biography or autobiography. Events are in **chronological order**, so you might want to use words such as

First / First of all…   **Then**…   **Next**…   **After that**…   **Eventually**…   **Finally**…

Your planning might be in the form of a timeline to help put your ideas in the right order. You might be asked to write a recount about a school trip. Remember, the reader doesn't want to hear about the boring bits, for example: 'At 9 o'clock we went to the toilet and washed our hands.' Skip to the more interesting parts! Be creative – do you have to start your opening paragraph with 'Yesterday we went on our class trip to…'? How about:

> As the coach rounded the corner to Lyme Park, we were amazed to see a herd of startled deer, which immediately leaped off in the opposite direction. In the distance we could see a lake shimmering in the autumn sun. I turned to face Emily and smiled. We had arrived!

Then you can start with the main part of the text:

> First of all, we visited ….

Keywords

Non-chronological ➤ Not in the order that something happens

Recount ➤ A report that retells an event that has happened

Chronological ➤ In the order that something happens

Choose a recent trip you have made with friends or family that you could write an interesting recount about.

1 What sort of report would you write if you wanted to tell someone about:

a. a visit to an art gallery?

b. nocturnal animals?

2 Write a timeline of your life so far. Think about key events: where and when you were born, school, family members, house move, hobbies and achievements.

Newspaper articles are a type of report. They should give the reader factual information, usually in the order events have happened. The big, bold headline is what hooks you in so it should be short, snappy and to the point. Some journalists use clever **puns** – a play on words – to get your attention:

MISSING DOG IS SPOTTED

ICE-CREAM WORKERS' WAGES FROZEN

Once you have read some examples of newspaper articles, you can start to plan your own. The features of a newspaper report are:

- headline (normally no more than seven words; try to use catchy words, alliteration, puns)
- **by-line** (who the article is by)
- lead paragraph – tells the reader **who**, **where**, **when**, **why** and **what**
- main body – tells the reader the details and how the events happened
- pictures with **captions**
- **sources** and / or eyewitnesses with **quotes**.

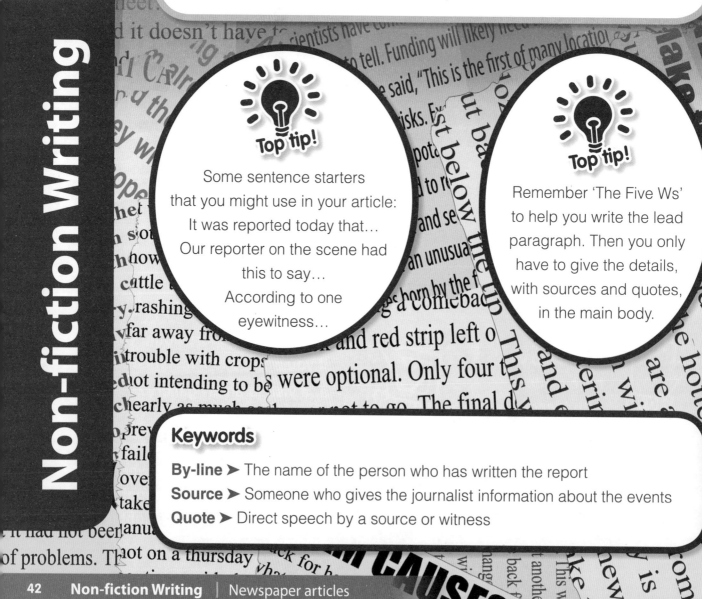

Top tip!

Some sentence starters that you might use in your article:
It was reported today that…
Our reporter on the scene had this to say…
According to one eyewitness…

Top tip!

Remember 'The Five Ws' to help you write the lead paragraph. Then you only have to give the details, with sources and quotes, in the main body.

Keywords

By-line ➤ The name of the person who has written the report

Source ➤ Someone who gives the journalist information about the events

Quote ➤ Direct speech by a source or witness

REMEMBER, REMEMBER, THE FIFTH OF NOVEMBER! *by Joe Welsh*

headline – catchy rhyme

by-line – name of the journalist

when?

what?

why?

who?

lead paragraph

where?

how?

quote from source

LAST night skies all over the country were on fire with 5th November fireworks displays. The celebration in memory of Guy Fawkes is one of Britain's oldest traditions but every year, sadly, someone gets injured or burned. When Cerys James set off with her parents to her local village bonfire, she didn't think she was going to be one of these statistics.

Although public safety had been made a top priority by the organisers of the display in Smalltown, Cheshire, and fireworks were lit at a safe distance, nobody could have imagined that a rogue Catherine Wheel would travel as far as it did, skimming Cerys's right ear before landing and burning out.

'It all happened so fast,' Cerys said. "I felt a searing pain on the top of my ear and screamed. In no time at all, a first aider appeared and applied an ice pack to my ear.'

where?

quote from another source

Luckily Cerys will be left with nothing more than a light scar on her ear.

'It could have been a lot worse,' admitted Bruce Jones, the display organiser. 'I am confident we did everything possible to keep the public safe but nobody could have planned for such a freak accident.'

5th November celebrations in Smalltown

picture and caption

summary

There have been no other reports of firework-related injuries in the local area, which was good news for fire services and hospital staff.

Have a go!

Write a newspaper article about a burglary that has occurred in a local school. A computer has been stolen and the thief got away. There is one source – the school caretaker – who tells you she / he definitely locked the school up the night before.

Test yourself

1 Name five main features of newspaper report writing.

Informal speech and writing

We tend to use **informal speech** when we are chatting to or writing to friends and family. It is a relaxed way of speaking. We might use **slang**, **abbreviations** and **colloquialisms**. **Standard English**, or correct grammar, can be used or, in very informal speech and writing, non-Standard English might be used (e.g. *I done*, *he were*)

Hey, how's it going? You goin' to footie practice?

Nah, can't be bothered. Got loadsa homework and Mum'll kill me if I get into more diffs with me maths.

We use informal writing when writing a postcard or a diary entry.

Fri 9th Sept

What an amazing day! Just chilled with Freya and Brogan then grabbed a pizza for tea. Think we'll head to the park tomorrow and hang out with Cassie and her crowd. It's gonna be wicked and I totally can't wait!

Formal speech and writing

If you were asked to write a letter to your Head Teacher, would you use the same tone, vocabulary and phrases as you would if you were writing to your best friend? Of course not! A letter to the Head Teacher would be quite **formal** in tone, using **Standard English**. You will hear examples of formal speech in presentations and debates, or when an interviewer introduces someone.

"A very warm welcome to you, Prince William. It's so good of you to spare the time to talk to us about your charity."

"It gives me great pleasure to introduce award-winning musician, Luke Lucas, to our school. I know we are all looking forward to hearing him play."

Keywords

Informal speech ➤ Relaxed, chatty way of speaking and writing

Slang ➤ Very informal language used when speaking to friends

Abbreviations ➤ Shortened word forms

Colloquialisms ➤ Expressions in informal, everyday language

Formal speech ➤ Using correct grammar and vocabulary

Standard English ➤ Using the rules of English grammar correctly

Formal writing

With so many people using texts and emails these days, letters have become a less popular form of communication. Look at the layout of this formal letter:

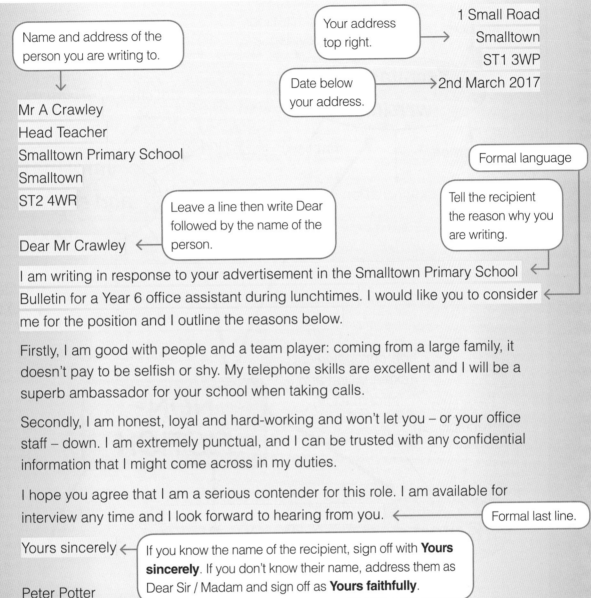

Name and address of the person you are writing to.

Your address top right.

1 Small Road
Smalltown
ST1 3WP

Date below your address.

2nd March 2017

Mr A Crawley
Head Teacher
Smalltown Primary School
Smalltown
ST2 4WR

Leave a line then write Dear followed by the name of the person.

Formal language

Tell the recipient the reason why you are writing.

Dear Mr Crawley

I am writing in response to your advertisement in the Smalltown Primary School Bulletin for a Year 6 office assistant during lunchtimes. I would like you to consider me for the position and I outline the reasons below.

Firstly, I am good with people and a team player: coming from a large family, it doesn't pay to be selfish or shy. My telephone skills are excellent and I will be a superb ambassador for your school when taking calls.

Secondly, I am honest, loyal and hard-working and won't let you – or your office staff – down. I am extremely punctual, and I can be trusted with any confidential information that I might come across in my duties.

I hope you agree that I am a serious contender for this role. I am available for interview any time and I look forward to hearing from you.

Formal last line.

Yours sincerely

If you know the name of the recipient, sign off with Yours sincerely. If you don't know their name, address them as Dear Sir / Madam and sign off as Yours faithfully.

Peter Potter

Listen to the news, then listen to a popular soap on the TV; how does the speech in each differ?

Have a go!

Test yourself

Listen up
19

① Rewrite these sentences using Standard English.

a. The Head's gotta give us a snow day!

b. It's, like, at least, like, a metre deep and me mum's car's broke.

c. OK, see wot happens but I'm so not goin' in!

d. Me an' all but betcha Tommo's ma makes 'im go!

This mind map will help you remember all the main points from this topic. Have a go at drawing your own mind map.

rhetorical questions

emotive language

statistics/ evidence

Persuasive writing

repetition

flattery

exaggeration

pictures and diagrams

contents page

bullet points

index

Information and explanation text

glossary

title

subheadings

bold or underlined key words

bold or coloured fonts

non-chronological (explanation and information)

recounts (chronological)

NON-FICTION

Reports

who, what, why, when, where, how

diaries

interviews

letters

Informal speech and writing

Formal speech and writing

newspaper reports

postcards

headline

by-line

sources

text messages

debates

quotes

chatting with friends and family

presentations

eyewitnesses

pictures and captions

in broadcasting

1 Write an information text about any city or foreign country of your choice.
Use the Internet or visit a library to research the information.
Present your information in a format of your choice, using the
plan below to help you.

Write your answer on a separate piece of paper. **(18 marks)**

Name of country:	
Geographical location	
Climate	
Culture	
Food and drink	
History	
Places of interest	

2 What is a 'source' in a newspaper article? **(1 mark)**

....

3 Name six features of persuasive writing. **(6 marks)**

....

....

....

....

....

....

4 List four techniques advertisers use to persuade you to buy
their products. **(4 marks)**

....

....

....

....

Types of nouns

Common nouns are naming words for people, places, animals and things. They also name things or ideas that cannot be seen or touched.

Proper nouns are the actual names of people, places, days of the week, months of the year, planets, titles of books, films, plays… it's a long list!

Common nouns

Here are some common nouns:

a **boy**   the **football**   a **dog**   the **table**   some **pens**

Some **nouns** name a group of things or people:

the Year 6 **class**   a **herd** of cows   a **murder** of crows

Other nouns are names of feelings or ideas, things you cannot see or touch:

anger   temptation   courage   love

Proper nouns

Proper nouns name a particular person, place or thing and **always** begin with a capital letter:

James   Thursday   Jupiter   The Hobbit   Germany

Keywords

Nouns ➤ Naming words for people, places, animals and things

Common nouns ➤ Nouns for people, animals and objects

Proper nouns ➤ Nouns that name things. They begin with a capital letter

Noun phrase ➤ A phrase where a noun is the main word

Expanded noun phrase ➤ A phrase with a noun as its main word with other words that tell us more about that noun

Pronoun ➤ A word that replaces a noun

Relative pronoun ➤ The words 'who', 'which', 'that', 'whose', 'where' and 'when' which introduce a relative clause

Relative clause ➤ A subordinate clause introduced by a relative pronoun

Possessive pronoun ➤ A word to show ownership

Noun phrases and expanded noun phrases

A **noun phrase** is a phrase that acts like a noun. The main word is a noun preceded by a determiner (see page 54).

> **the football**   **the clock**   **an apple**   **those trees**

Adding more information to a noun turns it into an **expanded noun phrase**.

> **The beautiful blue butterfly** landed on **the girl's pink hat**.

Pronouns

Pronouns can be used instead of nouns.

They are: I, you, he, she, it, we, they, me, him, her, us, them

> **Stella** visited a **castle** with her **mum** and **dad**. Her **mum** and **dad** said the **castle** was ancient.

We can replace the nouns in the second sentence with pronouns.   **They** said **it** was ancient.

Relative pronouns introduce a **relative clause** that says more about a noun. They are: that, which, who, whose, where, when

> clause that says more about the noun
>
> My best **friend**, **who** lives by the sea, is moving to London.
>
> relative pronoun
>
> noun

Possessive pronouns show ownership. They refer to something or someone previously mentioned.

They are: mine, yours, his, hers, its, ours, theirs

> my book
>
> That book is **mine**. The one on the shelf is **hers**. ← her book

Look around your home and make a list of five nouns you can see. Turn them first of all into noun phrases, then into expanded noun phrases.

❶ What nouns do the pronouns <u>it</u> and <u>them</u> refer to in this sentence?

Fred and Aisha stared into the distance. <u>It</u> seemed to pulsate with danger and filled <u>them</u> with fear.

❷ Rewrite these sentences, replacing the words underlined with possessive pronouns.

That bike isn't <u>your bike</u>! It's <u>my bike</u>!

Adjectives

Adjectives are words that give us more information about the noun in a sentence.

Stanley was a cat.

Stanley was a **black** and **white** cat with a **chubby** face and **pointy** ears.

Adjectives that compare two nouns usually end in **er**, but look what happens when the adjective has more than two syllables:

Adjective: **tall**:

Sam is **taller** than Aisha.

Adjective: **beautiful**:

Cinderella is **more beautiful** than her step-sisters.

Adjectives that **compare more than one noun** in a sentence usually end in **est**, but look what happens when the adjective ends in **y** or has more than two syllables:

Adjective: **short**:

Aisha is the **shortest** of all the children.

Adjective: **pretty**:

Orla has the **prettiest** dress in the whole performance.

Adjective: **impressive**:

Dan's hat is the **most impressive** hat of all.

Adverbs

Adverbs can give us more information about the verb. They can tell us about the **manner** in which an action is carried out.
Many of these end in the suffixes **ly** and **ally**.

quick**ly**   magic**ally**   hard   desperate**ly**   hungr**ily**   well

adverb		verb
Sam **suddenly collapsed** with exhaustion.		
verb	He had **tried hard** to win but without success.	adverb

Adverbs can also say more about an adjective in the sentence.

| adverb | Ushma was **quite excited** as she opened her presents. | adjective |

Adverbials and fronted adverbials

An **adverbial** is a word, phrase or clause that gives us more information about a verb (how, where, when, how often) or clause.

- slowly, quickly, crossly – **how**
- here, somewhere, far away – **where**
- soon, now, still, yesterday – **when**
- often, usually, occasionally – **how often**

> where → **Far**, **far away**, a dragon **still** roams the hills, **occasionally** breathing fire on the people below. ← how often → when

You can put the adverb or adverbial at the front, or start, of the sentence (called a **fronted adverbial**), followed by a comma.

> **Cautiously**, Tom crept into the gloomy darkness of the gaping cave.

Keywords

Adjective ➤ A word that describes a noun

Adverb ➤ A word that tells us more about a verb (how, where, when), an adjective, another adverb or a whole clause

Adverbial ➤ A word, phrase or clause that tells us more about a verb (how, where, when, how often) or clause

Fronted adverbial ➤ An adverb or adverbial coming at the start of a sentence

Top tip!
To help you find an adverb in a sentence, first find the verb.

Listen up
21

 **Have a go!** Listen to a documentary or news programme and make a note of as many adverbs and adverbials as you can hear.

 **Test yourself**

❶ Underline two adverbials in this sentence.

Erin wriggled through the gap and in a matter of minutes was free.

❷ Underline the adjectives in the sentence below.

Once the electric fence had been activated, even the most desperate animals couldn't escape.

Verb tenses

A **verb** tells you about an action, such as **run**, **skate**, **sing**. A verb can also tell you about a state of being, such as **to be**, **to love**, **to enjoy**.

Every sentence **must** have a verb. We can use the **present** or **past** tense to show whether something is happening now or has already happened.

Present and past tense

I **watch** television every evening.　　(**watch** is in the simple **present tense**)

The dog **was** absolutely wild.　　(**was** is in the simple **past tense**)

Present and past progressive tense

We can show that an action is / was continuous by using the progressive tenses.

I **am watching** television.　　(**present progressive**)

I **was watching** television.　　(**past progressive**)

Present and past perfect tense

We can show that an action is / was completed by using the perfect tenses.

The **present perfect** tense is formed from the present tense of the verb **have** and the past participle of the main verb. The **past perfect** tense is formed from the past tense of the verb **have** and the past participle of the main verb.

She **has played** outside all day so now she is tired.

(present tense of **have**; past participle of **play**)

Mum **had brought** the washing in before the rain started.

(past tense of **have**; past participle of **bring**)

Top tip!

To find the verb, first find the person, animal or thing in the sentence and see what they are **doing** or **being**.

Modal verbs

Modal verbs are verbs that change the meanings of other verbs. Here are some examples: will, shall, can, might, should, ought to, must, may, would, could.

As well as showing tenses, these verbs show where something is certain, probable, possible – or not.

Example sentence	Uncertain	Possible	Probable	Certain
I **may** be going swimming this evening. I **would** offer to take you with me but there **might** not be enough room in the car.	✓			
There **can** be as many as fifty children in the swimming pool at any given time.		✓		
Sam and Tom haven't eaten very much all day so they **must** be hungry by now.			✓	
The other team **will** be hard to beat so I **must** try hard to score a goal.				✓

Keywords

Verb ➤ A word for an action or state of being

Present ➤ A verb tense showing what is happening now

Past ➤ A verb tense showing what has happened

Present progressive ➤ A verb tense showing a continuous action in the present

Past progressive ➤ A verb tense showing a continuous action in the past

Present perfect ➤ A verb tense made from the present tense of 'have' + past participle of the main verb

Past perfect ➤ A verb tense made from the past tense of 'have' + past participle of the main verb

Modal verbs ➤ Verbs that can show possibility or likelihood

Have a go!

Write a diary entry about what you did at the weekend, using both ways of writing the past tense.

Test yourself

① Circle the most appropriate verb forms in these sentences:

a. I <u>drank/was drinking</u> my juice when the phone rang.

b. Just then the car <u>crashed/was crashing</u> into the brick wall.

c. I <u>eat/am eating</u> my supper every evening before I <u>watch/am watching</u> television.

d. I didn't think I <u>can/could</u> climb the mountain but I did!

e. After I <u>had practised / have practised</u> my spellings all week, I scored top marks in my test.

Listen up 22

Prepositions

Prepositions usually come before a noun or pronoun. They show the relationship between the noun or pronoun and other words in the clause or sentence. They often describe position or time.

The following are some common prepositions:

about	after	behind	in	of	since	under
above	at	by	into	off	through	up
across	before	during	near	on	to	with

This example uses prepositions indicating **position**:

Ben slid **behind** the sofa when his mum appeared **at** the door.

shows where Ben was in relation to the sofa

shows where his mum was in relation to the door.

This is an example of a preposition indicating **time**:

I haven't eaten **since** my breakfast this morning.

tells us how long it has been since the person last ate.

Determiners

A **determiner** is a word that comes before a noun to tell us whether the noun is specific (known, e.g. that cat) or general (unknown, e.g. some dogs).

Possessive determiners (e.g. my, your, his, her, its, our, their) show ownership of the noun which immediately follows.

My old aunt was invited to tea at **their** house.

The determiners the, a and an

- **the** is used when the noun is specified as known.
- **a** and **an** are used when the noun is specified as unknown.

The cat ran off and ended up on **an** ancient ship heading to **the** island.

| **the** is used because it refers to a specific cat (known) | **an** is used because it was just any ship (unknown) | **the** is used because it refers to a specific island (known) |

Keywords

Preposition ➤ Shows the relationship between the noun or pronoun and other words in the clause or sentence

Determiner ➤ A word that introduces a noun, such as 'the', 'a', 'some' and 'those'

Possessive determiner ➤ A determiner showing ownership of the noun that immediately follows

Have a go!

Create a set of instructions on how to get from the front door of your house into your bedroom. How many prepositions have you used?

Test yourself

1 Underline the determiners in the following sentences:

Some children were heading towards the beach when an adult came towards them waving a flag. It was the coastguard. He told them the weather had changed and they couldn't go in the sea. The children picked up their clothes and turned back to the path.

2 Underline the prepositions in the following sentences:

I went to my room and in it was the biggest mess imaginable! After I had cleared it, I went to the kitchen and sat at the table.

Conjunctions

A **conjunction** links two words, phrases or clauses together.

Conjunctions linking two words, phrases or clauses

Some conjunctions link two words, phrases or clauses together as a pair of equal importance. These are called **coordinating conjunctions**.

| and | but | or | nor | for | yet | so |

In these sentences, the words apples and oranges, and football and rugby, link together as a pair of equal importance.

Maeve likes apples **and** oranges.

Sami is good at neither football **nor** rugby.

In this sentence, the two clauses are linked together in equal importance:

Stanley is clever **but** he finds science challenging.

Keywords

Conjunction ➤ Links two words, phrases or clauses

Coordinating conjunction ➤ Links two words, phrases or clauses of equal importance

Subordinate clause ➤ A clause that depends on the main clause to make sense

Main clause ➤ A clause that can make sense as a sentence

Subordinating conjunction ➤ Joins a subordinate clause to a main clause

ADJECTIVE

ADVERB

LEARN ENGLISH

CONJUNCTION

PREPOSITION

NOUN   VERB   PRONOUN

Conjunctions that join a subordinate clause to a main clause

Some conjunctions join a **subordinate clause** to a **main clause**.
A subordinate clause starts with a **subordinating conjunction** and **does not** make sense on its own. A main clause **does** make sense on its own.

Here are some common conjunctions that join subordinate clauses to main clauses:

after   although   as   because   before   if   once   since   though
unless   until   when   whenever   where   whether   while

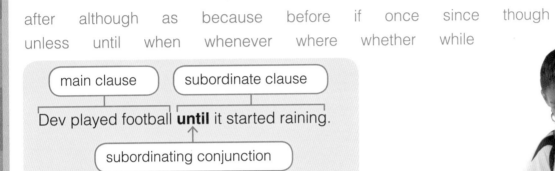

| main clause | subordinate clause |

Dev played football **until** it started raining.

↑
subordinating conjunction

Dev played football makes sense on its own.
Until it started raining doesn't make sense without the main clause.

The subordinate clause can come before the main clause:

| subordinate clause | main clause |

Although it was sunny, the children kept their coats on.

↑
subordinating conjunction

Top tip!

To identify the subordinate clause, find the conjunction in a sentence then read it followed by the clause that comes after it. Ask yourself, does the clause make sense on its own?

Have a go!

Choose a page from the book you are reading and copy some sentences containing subordinate clauses. Highlight the main clause in one colour and the subordinate clause in another.

Test yourself

❶ What is the difference between a main clause and a subordinate clause?

❷ Write eight conjunctions.

❸ Write two sentences, one containing the coordinating conjunction <u>but</u> and one containing the subordinating conjunction <u>unless</u>.

Statements

A **statement** is a sentence that contains some information. It usually ends in a full stop.

Our school has two playing fields**.**

Dominic is ten and likes rugby**.**

Questions

A **question** asks something and always ends with a question mark.

What time are you coming home**?**

Why do dogs wag their tails**?**

How is your mother**?**

Where have you been**?**

Sometimes we use sentence tags to turn a statement into a question:

You read that book I told you about, **didn't you?**

I've told you what happened to Amer yesterday, **haven't I?**

Keywords

Statement ➤ A sentence that gives information

Question ➤ A sentence that asks something

Commands

A **command** is a sentence instructing someone to do something. It contains a command verb and ends either in a full stop or an exclamation mark.

Eat your dinner now!

↑ command verb

Tell me your name, please.

↑ command verb

Exclamations

An **exclamation** is a sentence where you show feelings like fear, anger, excitement or happiness. It ends in an exclamation mark.

What a long day it has been**!**

How wonderful it would be to fly to the moon**!**

What a surprise I had when I opened the door**!**

How sad I was when my sister broke her arm**!**

What a lot of presents there are under the tree**!**

How beautiful the flowers look in Mum's vase**!**

Top tip! The noun **exclamation** comes from the verb **exclaim**. This should help you remember that an exclamation is followed by an exclamation mark!

Keywords

Command ➤ A sentence that gives an instruction

Exclamation ➤ A sentence where you show feelings like fear, anger, excitement or happiness.

Have a go! Write a set of instructions for making your favourite breakfast using command verbs.

Test yourself

① Write a suitable question for each of the following statements.

a. Horses eat hay.

b. Australia is in the Southern Hemisphere.

c. I go to bed at 9.00 pm.

Direct speech

When we want to tell the reader the exact words spoken by someone, we use **inverted commas** to show the beginning and the end of what they are saying. This is known as **direct speech**. Sometimes inverted commas are called **speech marks**.

> "I'm sure I've met you somewhere before," said Toby to the old gentleman.
>
> "Let me see – wasn't it last winter during the bad snowfall?" replied Mr Bates.

It's important to note that the comma, question mark, exclamation mark or full stop always comes inside the closing inverted commas.

> "I'll be back to help you with the gardening later**!**" called Dad. Under her breath, Mum muttered, "Later… when it's going to be raining**.**"

Keywords

Direct speech ➤ A sentence in inverted commas showing the exact words spoken by someone

Inverted commas / speech marks ➤ The punctuation at the start and end of direct speech

Using different verbs

There are many different verbs you can use to show the way in which the subject speaks in direct speech.

muttered	croaked	whispered	coughed
stuttered	screeched	agreed	admitted
uttered	shrieked	queried	begged
sighed	called	signalled	barked
cried	shouted	pointed	bellowed

Top tip!

If you are using speech bubbles in a storyboard, you do not need to use inverted commas.

Have a go!

Read a newspaper article and identify one example of direct speech and one example of reported speech (where someone reports what someone else has said).

Test yourself

1 Insert inverted commas into the following examples of direct speech:

a. There really isn't much point in packing a picnic, said Joe.

b. Well, it's not going to rain forever, Brogan pointed out. Look over there – I can see a patch of blue sky.

c. Good for you, said Joe grumpily. Do you really think the sun will come out though?

Active voice

Most writing is in the **active voice**.
Writing in the active voice just means that the subject of the sentence is doing something and the object (if there is one) of the sentence is what the subject is 'acting upon'.

Subject	Verb	Object	Ask yourself who or what is the subject 'acting upon'.
We	threw	some snowballs.	What were we throwing?
Ben	saw	the postman.	Who did Ben see?

Keywords

Active voice ➤ The subject of the sentence is doing or being; the object is having it done to them/it

Passive voice ➤ When the subject isn't carrying out the action but is being acted upon by someone or something

Parent tip!

Spot the passive voice! Look for the combination of the verb **to be** + the past form of the verb:
She **was attacked** (by the wasps).
She **is being praised** (by her teacher).

Top tip!

You will often see the passive voice being used in formal speech and writing, e.g. "I have been most warmly welcomed to this assembly by the Head Teacher."

Listen up
27

Passive voice

Where the subject is unknown or we want to put the attention on the person or thing affected by the action, we use the **passive voice**. We can change an active voice sentence to the passive voice by making the object the subject.

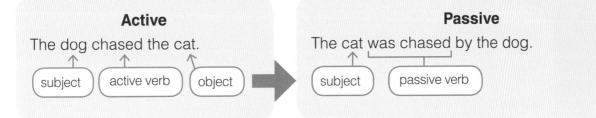

Active
The dog chased the cat.
subject — active verb — object

Passive
The cat was chased by the dog.
subject — passive verb

Sometimes, the object – the thing doing the action – isn't included in the passive voice:

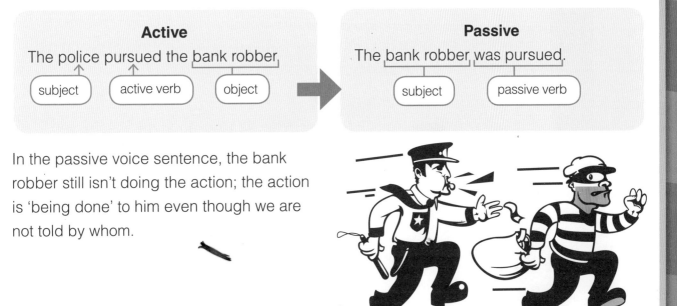

Active
The police pursued the bank robber.
subject — active verb — object

Passive
The bank robber was pursued.
subject — passive verb

In the passive voice sentence, the bank robber still isn't doing the action; the action is 'being done' to him even though we are not told by whom.

Have a go!

Turn this short paragraph from the active voice into the passive voice:

The teacher warned us not to hand our homework in late. She had reminded us many times before. The Head Teacher was definitely going to tell us off now!

Test yourself

❶ Say whether the following sentences are in the active or passive voice.

a. The children were swiftly rescued.

b. The older children pulled the youngest to safety first.

c. Everyone climbed onto the bus.

d. Some children were driven home by their parents.

Parenthesis is a word or phrase inserted into a sentence as an explanation or afterthought. The word or phrase sits inside a pair of **brackets**, **dashes** or **commas**. When you take the words in **parentheses** out of the sentence, what is left still makes sense.

Brackets

Brackets can come in the middle of a sentence or at the end.

> We ate the stale cake and said our goodbyes **(**we wouldn't be going back there again**)**.

> The children **(**who have only been swimming for a couple of years**)** did two lengths in the charity swim.

> It was only eight o'clock **(**I know because I looked at my watch**)**, yet the town was in complete darkness.

Use a range of punctuation marks in your writing to show parenthesis. It will make it more interesting to read.

Top tip!

Dashes

A pair of **dashes** can also indicate parenthesis.

> The teachers were very cross – not surprisingly – and spoke to the whole school about poor behaviour.

> Finding a way across the swollen river – difficult even on a calm day – was proving almost impossible.

Commas

Commas can also be used to show parenthesis.

> Marco, tightrope walker extraordinaire, amazed the crowd with his daring agility.

> The Browns, a family we met on holiday, helped us to put up our tent.

The words in parentheses give us extra information. They are sometimes relative clauses with the relative pronoun left out. The sentence above could have been written:

> The Browns, <u>who were a family we met on holiday</u>, helped us to put up our tent.

Have a go!

Insert suitable parentheses in this sentence:

We went white-water rafting an often dangerous sport and thoroughly enjoyed ourselves.

Test yourself

❶ Rewrite these sentences, inserting a word, phrase or clause in the gaps using appropriate parentheses.

    a. I couldn't be bothered to go swimming .... so I stayed at home.

    b. We were amazed by the trapeze artists at the circus ....

    c. Having been there on holiday before .... we knew our way around.

    d. Houdini .... featured on a TV documentary last night.

An **apostrophe** looks like a comma but does not sit on the line – it sits at the same height as inverted commas.

We can use it in two different ways:

- to show **possession** – in other words, to show that something belongs to someone
- to show **omission**, where a letter (or letters) has been left out – in other words **contraction**, to show where a word (or words) has been made shorter.

Apostrophes for possession

The rules for using an apostrophe to show possession are:

- singular nouns – add an apostrophe after the word followed by an **s**
- plural nouns ending in **s** – add only an apostrophe after the final **s**
- proper nouns ending in **s** – add an apostrophe followed by an **s**.

> apostrophe after lady (singular noun) followed by **s**

The lady's handbag was found by the police after they had found **the thieves' footsteps** in the mud.

> apostrophe after the **s** in thieves (plural noun)

James's rucksack was full of books.

> apostrophe after the **s** in James (proper noun)

Top tip!

There's an important exception to the possession rule! The word **it's** always means **it is**, so for possession it does **not** get an apostrophe.

The dog wagged its tail. ✓

If it was **it's**, the sentence would read:

The dog wagged it is tail. ✗

This doesn't make sense at all!

Keywords

Apostrophe ➤ A punctuation mark used to show omission, contraction or possession

Possession ➤ Ownership

Omission ➤ Where a letter or letters have been left out

Contraction ➤ Where a word has been made shorter

Listen up
29

Apostrophes for contraction or omission

When we speak or write informally, we often use contractions. These are words that have been shortened by omitting, or leaving out, a letter or letters.

The following are common contractions:

I am	I'm		will not	won't
she is	she's		cannot	can't
we have	we've		it is	it's
they are	they're		we will	we'll
does not	doesn't		shall not	shan't

It's important that you position the apostrophe in the correct place – where the missing letter or letters would be.

we will →   it is →   It will →   because →

We'll have to remember it's Dad's birthday next week. It'll be fun to surprise him, 'cause he's bound to forget.

↑ he is

Parent tip!

If someone's name ends in **s**, such as James, an apostrophe followed by an **s** can be used in the normal way.
I enjoy reading Dickens's novels.

Words ending in **double s**, such as princess, follow the normal rule too.
The prince took the princess's hand.

Have a go!

On a piece of paper, make a list of people's names on the left hand side then pair them up with items you can see around the house, showing possession. For example: Sarah's lampshade, Chris's picture... etc.

Test yourself

❶ Insert the missing apostrophes in these sentences.

Jakes mums chicken pie wasnt the best. Shed burnt its edges as shed left it in the oven too long. They shouldve gone out to Charlies Chippy, thought Jake.

Grammar and Punctuation

This mind map will help you remember all the main points from this topic. Have a go at drawing your own mind map.

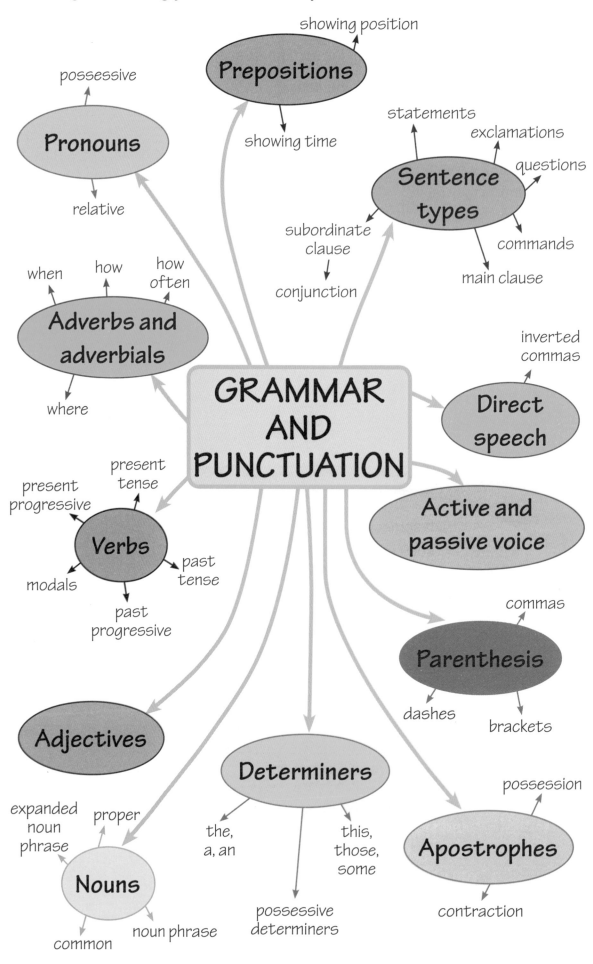

showing position

Prepositions

showing time

possessive

Pronouns

relative

statements

exclamations

questions

Sentence types

commands

subordinate clause

main clause

conjunction

when   how   how often

Adverbs and adverbials

where

inverted commas

Direct speech

present tense

present progressive

Verbs

modals

past tense

past progressive

GRAMMAR AND PUNCTUATION

Active and passive voice

commas

Parenthesis

dashes

brackets

Adjectives

Determiners

the, a, an

this, those, some

possessive determiners

possession

Apostrophes

contraction

expanded noun phrase

proper

Nouns

common

noun phrase

1 Write the nouns in the box below in the correct columns of the table. **(3 marks)**

hand	dog	strength	Antarctica	fear
flock	flower	July	house	despair
Prince George	Jupiter	bravery	pity	United Kingdom

Proper nouns	Common nouns	
	Nouns we can see or touch	**Nouns we can't see or touch**

2 Write this present tense sentence in the past tense. **(1 mark)**

I eat my dinner quickly.

....

3 Underline the modal verbs in these sentences.

a. My mother couldn't finish the horror story. **(1 mark)**

b. The heating has been on so the house must be warm now. **(1 mark)**

c. Would it be possible to leave the theatre now? **(1 mark)**

4 Write a sentence which contains a main clause and a subordinate clause. **(1 mark)**

....

....

5 Underline the coordinating conjunctions in this short passage. **(2 marks)**

We had salad and bread for tea but nothing at bedtime. The next morning we were tired and hungry. There was some cereal on the table yet no sign of any milk.

6 Underline the five pronouns in the sentence below. **(2 marks)**

Charlotte hurt her finger at the park and she had to have it bandaged. The nurse praised her for being brave and she gave her a special plaster.

7 Underline the five adverbs and adverbials in these sentences. **(2 marks)**

Soon Harry reached the cellar where he stumbled awkwardly over a carelessly discarded pizza box. Trying not to make a sound, Harry crept with great caution into the gloom…

A **prefix** is a string of letters added to the beginning of a word to turn it into another word.

Some prefixes change the word so that it is opposite or negative in meaning but they don't change the spelling.

Prefixes dis and mis

The prefixes **dis** and **mis** usually give the word a negative meaning.

tasteful ⟶ **dis**tasteful

guided ⟶ **mis**guided

I agreed with Claire but Katie **dis**agreed with us both.

Prefixes im and in

The prefixes **im** and **in** also give a negative meaning. If the **root word** starts with **m** or **p**, use **im**, but otherwise use **in**.

definite ⟶ **in**definite

perfect ⟶ **im**perfect

measurable ⟶ **im**measurable

Ben's art project was **in**complete.

im possible

Prefixes il, ir and un

The prefixes **il** and **ir** give an opposite meaning when placed in front of a word. If the root word starts with **l**, use the prefix **il**; if the root word starts with **r**, generally use **ir**. The prefix **un** also gives a negative or opposite meaning.

legal ⟶ **il**legal (It would be very hard to say 'irlegal'!)

replaceable ⟶ **ir**replaceable (It would be quite hard to say 'ilreplaceable'!)

tie ⟶ **un**tie

Top tip!

Other prefixes include:

- **de**, which indicates removal or reversal (e.g. **de**compose).
- **over**, which can imply 'too much' (e.g. **over**run).
- **re**, which indicates 'again' or 'back' (e.g. **re**type, **re**wind).

Prefixes from Latin and Greek

Some prefixes have their origins in Greek or Latin, such as **bi** meaning 'two', **tele** meaning 'far off' and **super** meaning 'greater or above'. With these, you just need to learn their meaning to help you work out the meaning of the whole word.

bi + cycle = bicycle	(two wheels)
tele + scope = telescope	(makes far off things appear closer)
super + market = supermarket	(a big shop)
anti + freeze = antifreeze	(prevents water freezing)
auto + biography = autobiography	(an account of someone's life, written by that person)

Keywords

Prefix ➤ A string of letters added to the start of a word to change its meaning

Root word ➤ A word in its own right, without a prefix or a suffix

Top tip!

Make the link to the number 2 when you come across words starting with the prefix **bi**, for example, binoculars, biannual, bilingual.

Have a go!

What do the prefixes <u>auto</u> and <u>aqua</u> mean? Write some words starting with these prefixes and write their meanings.

Test yourself

❶ Unravel these anagrams to find words starting with <u>il</u> or <u>ir</u>.

a. sister liberi

b. little aire

c. rail ration

d. glaci olli

Listen up 31

A **suffix** is a letter or a string of letters added to the end of a root word, changing or adding to its meaning.

Suffixes s and es

The suffix **s** can be added to most nouns to form the plural.

dog ⟶ dog**s**

If the noun ends in **ch**, **sh**, **ss** or **x**, the suffix **es** is added.

church ⟶ church**es**

wish ⟶ wish**es**

kiss ⟶ kiss**es**

fox ⟶ fox**es**

Suffixes able and ably

You can add **able** to a root word to make an adjective.
If the word ends in **ce** or **ge**, you need to keep the **e** when you add the suffix.

> The weather could change today.
>
> The weather is looking quite change**able** today.

You can add **ably** to a root word to make an adverb.

consider ⟶ consider**ably**

> There is a considerable amount of litter in the park.
>
> The litter in the park has got consider**ably** worse.

Suffixes ible and ibly

You can add **ible** to a root word to make an adjective.

sense ⟶ sens**ible**

> That dog has no sense.
>
> That dog isn't sens**ible**.

You can add **ibly** to a root word to make an adverb.

force ⟶ forc**ibly**

Some words do not have an obvious root because they come from other languages, such as Latin or Greek. For example, **possibly** – there's no such thing as a 'poss'!

Keyword

Suffix ➤ A letter or a string of letters added to the root word to change or add to its meaning

Top tip!

The suffixes **ful** and **less** can also be used to form adjectives, e.g. hope ⟶ hope**ful**
care ⟶ care**less**

Suffixes cial and tial

The suffixes **cial** and **tial** can be added to root words to make adjectives. The suffix **cial** is mainly used after a vowel and the suffix **tial** after a consonant.

office ⟶ offi**cial**
essence ⟶ essen**tial**

'Spatial' is an exception: can you think of any more?

Suffixes cious and tious

The suffixes **cious** and **tious** can also be used to make adjectives. The suffix **cious** is usually used if the root word ends in **ce**. If the word ends in **tion**, then the suffix **tious** is used.

grace ⟶ gra**cious**
caution ⟶ cau**tious**

Suffixes from Greek

The suffixes **logy**, **phone**, **phobia** and **meter** have their origins in the Greek language.

zoology

telephone

claustrophobia

perimeter

Support your child to make connections with other words that have the Greek suffixes **logy**, **phone**, **phobia** and **meter**.

Parent tip!

Suffixes ment, ness and er

The suffixes **ment**, **ness** and **er** can be used to form nouns.

enjoy ⟶ enjoy**ment**
happy ⟶ happi**ness**
teach ⟶ teach**er**

Suffixes ate, ise and ify

The suffixes **ate**, **ise** and **ify** can be used to convert nouns or adjectives into verbs.

participant ⟶ particip**ate**
agony ⟶ agon**ise**
solid ⟶ solid**ify**

Have a go! Use a dictionary or the Internet to find out the meanings of the Greek suffixes <u>meter</u> and <u>phobia</u>.

Test yourself

1 Add either <u>cial</u> or <u>tial</u> to the following words, remembering to apply the rule.

a. residence
b. face
c. finance
d. influence

The rule 'i before e except after c, but only when it rhymes with bee'

Most words follow the rule **i before e**.

piece
field
shield

If the **ee** sound follows a **soft c**, the spelling is **ei**.

deceit
receipt
deceive

There are of course some exceptions:

- Some words have an **ei** spelling, despite not coming after a **soft c**; they have an **ay** sound.

eight
weight
beige

- Other words have an **ei** spelling but an **ee** sound.

weird
protein
caffeine

Top tip!

Say the rule '**i before e except after c, but only when it rhymes with bee**' as if it is a rhyme. It will help you remember it. Do not forget to learn the exceptions to the rule though.

Listen up 32

Words ending in fer

When you add a suffix to a word ending in **fer**, it is helpful to say the word aloud to identify where the **stress** or **emphasis** falls so you can decide whether you need to double the **r**.

If the **syllable fer** is still stressed after the suffix is added, the **r** is doubled.

refer ⟶ re<u>fer</u>ral (stressed so double **r**)

prefer ⟶ pre<u>fer</u>ence (not stressed so single **r**)

transfer ⟶ trans<u>fer</u>red (stressed so double **r**)

infer ⟶ in<u>fer</u>ence (not stressed so single **r**)

The manager signed the player who had trans**ferr**ed from another team, despite his pre**fer**ence to stay put.

Silent letters

Some letters that were sounded hundreds of years ago are no longer sounded today. These **silent letters**, however, often remain in the words. The word **knight**, for example, used to be pronounced with a hard **k** sound. The study of the origin of words, and the way in which their meanings and sounds have changed throughout history, is called **etymology**.

Look at these words containing silent letters.

knot   **g**narl   **g**nome   We**d**nesday

Letter string ough

The letter string **ough** is one of the trickiest to spell, especially as it can be used to spell a few different sounds.

Can you find the sounds **oh**, **aw**, **uff**, **ow** and **off** in this sentence?

> Alth**ough** Oliver th**ough**t the sea was r**ough**, he was a t**ough** sailor who pl**ough**ed on, despite his bad c**ough**.

Keywords

Stress ➤ When you either increase the vowel length or loudness of the syllable, or both

Emphasis ➤ Stress

Syllable ➤ A single, unbroken sound containing at least one vowel

Silent letter ➤ A letter that is no longer pronounced

Etymology ➤ The origin of words

Top tip! Seeing the relationship between words in the same word families can help you with spelling, e.g. medicine – medical – medication.

Have a go! Create a table with the headings:

| ei after soft c |
| i before e |
| ei with ay sound |
| ei with ee sound |

Find as many words for each column as you can.

Test yourself

❶ Circle the correct spelling of the underlined words.

a. The passenger <u>preffered</u> / <u>preferred</u> <u>transferring</u> / <u>transfering</u> her suitcase using the <u>unwieldy</u> / <u>unweildy</u> trolley.

b. I kept <u>receiving</u> / <u>recieving</u> letters with a <u>wierd</u> / <u>weird</u> stamp advertising <u>abseiling</u> / <u>absieling</u> events.

Homophones

Homophones are words that sound the same but have different spellings and different meanings.

> hair and hare

If you do not spell these words correctly, it could be confusing for the reader.

> Standing **here** I could not **hear** the **whales' wails**.

Here are some common homophones.

two	to	too
groan	grown	
reins	reigns	rains
there	their	they're
we're	weir	
altar	alter	
isle	aisle	
weather	whether	
ascent	assent	
draft	draught	
aloud	allowed	
cereal	serial	
rowed	road	

Near homophones

Near homophones are homophones that do not sound exactly the same but they are similar enough that people often misspell them.

> The park is very **quiet** this morning, though it's still **quite** early.

Affect and effect are near homophones that are commonly misused.

- affect – usually a verb
- effect – usually a noun

> verb
> ↓
> The weather can **affect** some people's mood. A sunny day can have such a positive **effect**.
> ↑
> noun

To help you remember practice / practise:

- practice with a **c** is a **n**oun; **c** comes before **n** in the alphabet
- practise with an **s** is a **v**erb; **s** comes before **v** in the alphabet.

Listen up 33

Do bear in mind regional accents when discussing whether two words sound similar or the same!

Keywords

Homophones ➤ Words that sound the same but have different spellings and different meanings

Near homophones ➤ Words that sound almost the same as another

How many homophones can you think of?

Have a go!

Test yourself

1 Choose the correct word from these near homophones.

a. The new Head Teacher was soon <u>accepted/excepted</u> by the staff.

b. The new Head Teacher had an amazing <u>affect/effect</u> on the children.

This mind map will help you remember all the main points from this topic. Have a go at drawing your own mind map.

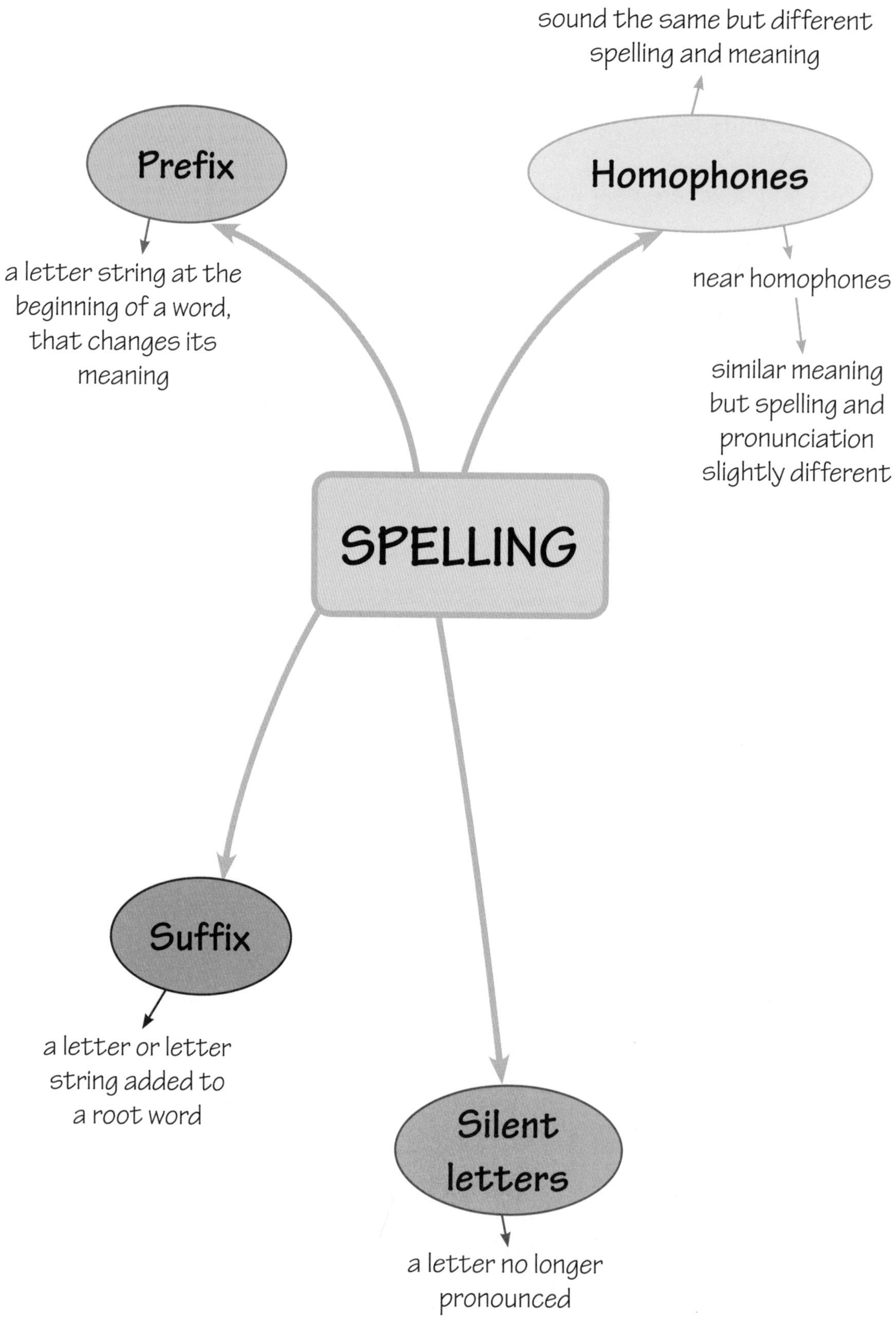

sound the same but different spelling and meaning

Homophones

Prefix

a letter string at the beginning of a word, that changes its meaning

near homophones

similar meaning but spelling and pronunciation slightly different

SPELLING

Suffix

a letter or letter string added to a root word

Silent letters

a letter no longer pronounced

1 Use an appropriate prefix to change the meaning of these words. **(4 marks)**

happy	....
understand	....
appropriate	....
polite	....

2 Underline the two incorrect words in these sentences then write the correct homophones.

a. We eight our pairs and went out to play. **(1 mark)**

....

b. They're hare has been cut very short. **(1 mark)**

....

3 Use an appropriate suffix to change these words into adjectives. **(4 marks)**

influence	....
division	....
horror	....
present	....

4 Spell the underlined words, which have been written as they sound, correctly.

(2 marks)

We have only <u>brawt</u> our <u>ruff</u> sketches, <u>althow</u> if we have <u>enuff</u> time we <u>awt</u> to be able to complete them.

....

....

5 Circle the correct homophone in each sentence.

a. My little sister created a **seen / scene** when we were leaving the zoo. **(1 mark)**

b. We had an excellent **dessert / desert** in the restaurant last night. **(1 mark)**

6 Underline the correctly spelled word in brackets in the sentences below.

a. Some cracks have appeared in my (ceiling/cieling). **(1 mark)**

b. My parents (recieved/received) my school report last night. **(1 mark)**

c. The Latin expression *carpe diem* means '(seize/sieze) the day'. **(1 mark)**

Practise speaking out loud in front of a mirror. Use your hands and arms for expression and articulate your words clearly.

Top tip!

Listen up 34

Reading out loud

It can be quite daunting to read aloud in class because you feel you are the centre of attention. Here are some tips to help you feel more confident:

- Use the punctuation as signposts that tell you when to pause or stop to take a breath
- Read slowly – if you rush, you will 'trip' over words and become more flustered
- Pretend that the class has left the room and you are reading out loud to yourself!
- Don't hide your face behind the text – your voice will be muffled and you won't appear confident
- Remember: your teacher will support you with tricky words – just ask!

Delivering a presentation

Sometimes you will be asked to present something you have been working on to an audience. This might be a group, your class or even the whole school in an assembly.

If you can, film yourself and observe how you deliver your presentation, making improvements to your delivery all the time.

It might be appropriate to use pictures, props or ICT to keep your audience interested.

It's always very impressive to do a presentation without reading from the text; try using cue cards with the main points written on them to jog your memory.

Use devices such as exaggeration, repetition, emotive language and rhetorical questions to help put your point of view across.

Body language

It's important to think about **body language** when addressing an audience. Use expression when you are talking; your audience will soon lose interest if you use a **monotone** (one tone) voice throughout your presentation. Change the pace and volume of your voice too, depending on the effect you are trying to create. You might want to pause at the end of a rhetorical question:

> Change your voice to a louder volume here for emphasis.

Do you **really** want the next generation of children to suffer the side-effects of radiation emitted from mobile phones?

> You could pause here for 'dramatic effect' before going on to your next sentence.

If you want to really emphasise a point, you could **gesticulate** (use gestures) or pound the table with your fist.

> You could shake your head here or wave your hand in the air for emphasis.

I cannot say it often enough: animal cruelty is a disgrace and must be stamped out!

> Pound table on this word to drive your point home.

Keywords

Body language ➤ Using your body to get your point across or get the audience's attention
Monotone ➤ Using no expression, so your voice has only one tone
Gesticulate ➤ To use gestures to emphasise your point

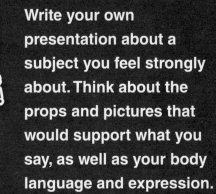

Have a go! Write your own presentation about a subject you feel strongly about. Think about the props and pictures that would support what you say, as well as your body language and expression.

Test yourself
❶ What is a monotone voice?
❷ How can body language be used in delivering a speech?
❸ What might you show to an audience when delivering a presentation?

Drama

Acting is a great way to gain confidence in speaking to an audience. Some quite shy people suddenly become extrovert, expressive characters with booming voices when they are performing in a play.

Use expression and body language when you are acting otherwise you will come across as 'wooden' or expressionless.

Role play

When you are asked by your teacher to use role play to gain a better understanding of a character or a situation, are you a 'shrinking violet'? Do you let the others in the group take the lead roles while you happily make props? It's important to push yourself out of your comfort zone and increase your self-confidence and self-belief.

Hot-seating and interviewing

Hot-seating is a type of role play. Someone pretends to be the person you want to find out information about; usually a famous person. You could be put in the hot-seat as Winston Churchill and answer questions about World War II. It's a bit like an interview, where relevant and interesting questions are asked, designed to get the most out of the interviewee.

When writing interview questions, remember that 'closed' questions won't get the most interesting answers; the answers to 'closed' questions are generally 'yes' or 'no' or one-word answers. Try to ask 'open' questions so that the interviewee or person in the hot-seat has got to give more detailed answers.

Listen up 35

Top tip!

Ask open questions to get a more detailed response from the interviewee.

Read this interview with the actors from the film of *The Railway Children*. Look at how the interviewer is able to draw a lot of information out of the three children.

Have you read E. Nesbit's book?

JEMIMA: I read it when I was very young as it's one of those classic books everyone reads. I read it again when I was auditioning for the part of Bobbie so I could research the character.

CLARE: I once started to read it but didn't finish it but then, when I got the part of Phyllis, I had to complete a book-reading exercise for school so I read it then.

JACK: I haven't read it all, but I have heard it on tape and I've seen the 1970 film.

How easy was it to play your characters?

JEMIMA: It's easy now, but at first I was worried, because playing a twelve-year-old in the early 1900s is very different. They were very much children then until they were quite a lot older.

CLARE: Phyllis is pretty easy to play, because she's quite young and hasn't learnt much about the world yet. She doesn't have any major speeches using large, old-fashioned words.

JACK: Playing Peter is quite straightforward. I think he's trying to be grown up and be the man of the house. He's not really that big, but would like to take control.

What similarities have you noticed between your characters and yourselves?

JEMIMA: Bobbie is lovely and she's one of those people you admire and want to be like. She is very sweet and gentle with her brother and sister. She's very amusing, trying to be adult and mature. I'd like to think we were similar, but really I don't think so! Jack, Clare and I feel like real brother and sisters, which is nice. I definitely feel like their older sister. But no, I don't think I'm really like Bobbie at all.

How does wearing the period costumes help towards playing the character?

JEMIMA: It really, really helps! The minute you've got your costume on your movements are restricted. It makes me feel like a little doll, which makes me feel younger and helps with the part.

JACK: Most of the costumes are alright, but at the moment I am having problems with this stiff collar! It's kind of hard to breathe sometimes. I think wearing the costumes does help you to focus.

Choose someone you admire greatly and would like to interview. Write open questions that you think would reveal the most interesting information about that person.

1. What are closed questions?
2. What is hot-seating?
3. What is one positive aspect to taking up drama?

Speaking and Listening

This mind map will help you remember all the main points from this topic. Have a go at drawing your own mind map.

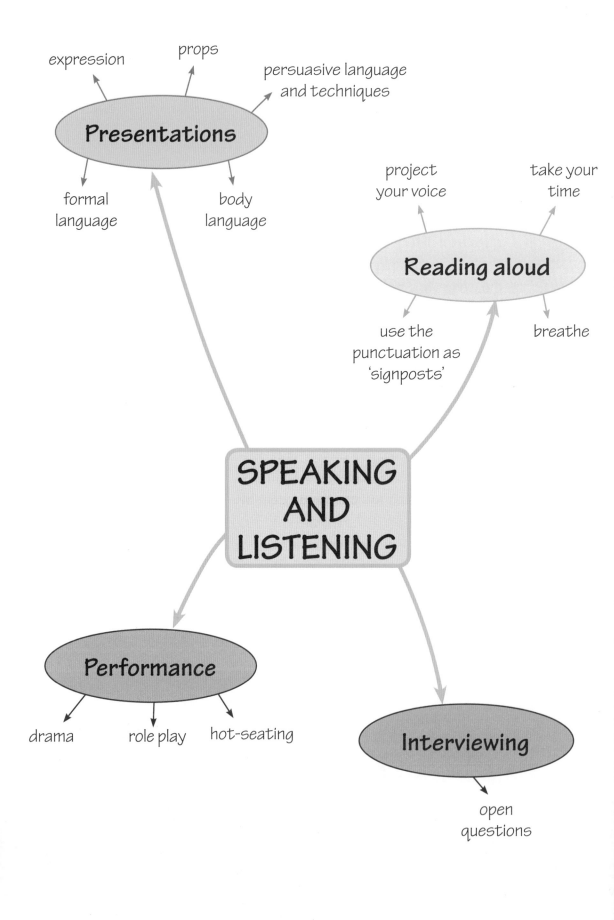

expression

props

persuasive language and techniques

Presentations

formal language

body language

project your voice

take your time

Reading aloud

use the punctuation as 'signposts'

breathe

SPEAKING AND LISTENING

Performance

drama   role play   hot-seating

Interviewing

open questions

1 Here are some facts about Nelson Mandela. Write **six** open questions that you would like to ask him in an interview if he were alive today.   **(6 marks)**

- He was sentenced to life in prison for fighting against apartheid.
- He was imprisoned on Robben Island.
- While he was in prison, he was told that if he stopped his acts of violence, he would be allowed to go free. He did not agree to this.
- He was in prison for over 27 years.
- In 1968, both his mother and son died. However, he was not allowed to attend their funerals.
- In 1994, he became the first president of South Africa to be elected by a democratic system, and the first black president.
- One of his hobbies was boxing.
- He was a Christian.

1. ....

2. ....

3. ....

4. ....

5. ....

6. ....

2 Imagine you have been asked to talk in assembly about healthy eating. Write a short presentation on the lines below, then present it to a friend or family member.   **(6 marks)**

....

....

....

....

....

....

1 Answer the questions below about this extract from a piece of persuasive writing.

> Despite the obvious risk to their children's health, many parents are happy to supply them with the mobile phone of their choice. Mobile phones emit a certain amount of radiation, which can be harmful to the user. There is the additional risk that constantly looking at small text on a small screen can be damaging to a child's eyesight.
>
> On the other hand, mobiles are useful: parents can maintain contact with their children and obviously they are beneficial in emergency situations when having one, or not, could mean the difference between life and death.
>
> Parents should think carefully before purchasing a mobile phone for their child.

a. According to the writer, what is one health risk from using a mobile phone? **(1 mark)**

....

b. What adverb in the first paragraph means 'always'? **(1 mark)**

....

c. Why might a mobile phone be useful in emergency situations? **(1 mark)**

....

2 Read this extract about the Orient Express and then answer the questions.

> The Venice Simplon Orient Express is the world's most famous luxury train. It has been used by the rich and famous since its first journey in 1883. Glamour, elegance and style apply to both the train and its passengers.
>
> On board, passengers have their own personal stewards attending to their every need. Wood-panelled compartments provide private sitting rooms by day and luxurious bedrooms by night.
>
> A dining car is laid out with the finest crystal glasses, table linen and cutlery awaiting the service of wonderful food produced by French chefs.
>
> In the evening, passengers wearing fine gowns and suits gather to sip drinks as they chat or listen to the piano in the bar.
>
> All this takes place as the train snakes its way across Europe and if the quality of life inside the train becomes too much, the passengers can simply look through the window at some of the finest scenery the continent has to offer.
>
> A journey on the Orient Express is an extraordinary one. Wealthy passengers travel in luxury through a rich and varied landscape on what is seen by many to be the most romantic journey in the world.

a. The Orient Express has many luxuries. According to the text, where can these be found on the train? Draw a line to match the objects on the left to the places on the right. **(2 marks)**

a piano ⬭   ⬭ in the compartments

wood panelling ⬭   ⬭ in the dining car

fine views ⬭   ⬭ in the bar

finest crystal glasses ⬭   ⬭ through the window

b. Why does the author use the word 'snakes' to describe the train's journey across Europe? **(1 mark)**

....

....

c. If you were a passenger on the Orient Express, who would you ask if you needed anything? **(1 mark)**

....

3 Read the passage below about a climber in a life-threatening situation and answer the questions.

> Clinging desperately to the frozen rope, I focused on rejecting any thought of death; yet the longer I dangled there, limp and helpless, the more certain it seemed that I would meet my end. The icy wind cut into my face, blasting my lips numb, caking my eyelashes with thick frost. What was Simon doing up there? Suddenly the rope vibrated then shook violently, causing me to glance in horror at the crevasse yawning below. In blind panic, I felt for the hard metal of the karabiner – yes, it was secure. But for how long could I continue swinging there? Sleep beckoned... not long now...

a. What is the narrator trying not to think about? **(1 mark)**

....

b. How does the narrator use personification to show the pain the climber is suffering due to the weather conditions? **(1 mark)**

....

....

c. Why does the climber 'glance in horror at the crevasse' below? **(1 mark)**

....

d. What do you think a 'karabiner' is? **(1 mark)**

....

4 Replace the underlined word or words in each sentence with the correct **possessive pronoun**. **(1 mark)**

These books belong to him. These books are ....

This dog is owned by our neighbours. This dog is ....

That car belongs to us. That car is ....

5 Tick the sentence that uses the correct **plural**. **(1 mark)**

Have you seen those peoples swimming? ☐

I saw six gooses crossing the river. ☐

The farm dog rounded up all the sheep. ☐

We saw the thiefs leaving the bank. ☐

6 Write the underlined words in the correct place in the table. **(1 mark)**

The <u>dedicated</u> <u>group</u> went for a <u>brisk</u> <u>walk</u>.

Noun	Adjective

7 Complete the sentence with an appropriate **adverb**. **(1 mark)**

The children waded .... across the stream.

8 a. Write a sentence using the word <u>fire</u> as a noun. **(1 mark)**

....

....

b. Write a sentence using the word <u>fire</u> as a verb. **(1 mark)**

....

....

9 Draw a line to match each sentence to the correct **determiner**. Use each determiner only **once**. **(1 mark)**

Sentence	Determiner
The children stood before .... castle.	a
There was .... ancient gate with huge hinges.	the
With .... mighty heave, they pushed it open.	an

10 Circle the **two conjunctions** in the sentence below. **(1 mark)**

Hassan went to the doctor because he had a sore throat and a temperature.

11 Change these sentences from the **active voice** to the **passive voice**.

(1 mark)

Mum and Dad took us to the seaside on the bus.

....

....

The lady who owned the hotel showed us around.

....

....

12 Circle the **object** in the sentence below. **(1 mark)**

Joseph quickly finished his homework.

13 Insert **inverted commas** in the correct places in the dialogue below. **(1 mark)**

We haven't got all day, Brogan said impatiently. Hurry up!

14 Underline the **subordinate clause** in each sentence below. **(1 mark)**

As we were driving to school, we noticed that someone had fallen on the footpath.

When we arrived at the swimming pool, the attendants told us it was closed.

The park, which had been closed for improvements, reopened at the weekend.

15 Insert the missing **comma** in the correct place in the sentence below. **(1 mark)**

As he walked towards the church Tom was aware of someone following him.

READING

Test Yourself Questions

page 5

1. A blurb gives a brief overview of the book.
2. a. Fiction is stories that have been made up.
   b. Non-fiction is information and facts.
3. If you are empathising with someone you are understanding and sharing their feelings.
4. 'Genre' is the type or kind of writing.

page 7

1. Personification is when an inanimate object is given human characteristics.
2. a. a nightingale
   b. a surging swell of boiling liquid
   c. burning lava
   d. a cucumber

page 9

1. a. My fine time in Hawaii soon went by.
   b. Creeping up past my knees, the sea was three feet deep.
2. a. 'Pop' went Pippa's pink party balloon.
   b. The gentle Splish-Splash of the Surging Sea Sent me to Sleep.

page 11

1. The turf she was walking on was soft so it wouldn't cause her any discomfort.
2. a. 'snaked' tells us that the crack was long and not straight; it was like a snake. It also implies a sense of danger.
   b. 'came to a halt'

page 13

1. a. That there are stars in the sky and it's night.
   b. The repetition of 'riding' helps you visualise the continuous action of the highwayman riding in the distance then getting closer to the inn.
2. a. It has rained so hard, that the water has become 'muddy' and there is so much of it that it is almost tidal like the sea.
   b. 'Like a river'

page 15

1. To explain where actors and props should be, what is going on around them and how they should say something.
2. The story of a play is told through dialogue and sometimes a narrator.
3. 'Exit stage right' means the actor or actors should leave the stage on the right-hand side.
4. Answers will vary. A description that shows Monika as persistent/funny/lazy/determined/ good relationship with her dad.

page 17

1. title; subheadings; pictures (with captions) or diagrams (annotated); contents page; index; glossary

page 19

1. a. 'The norm' means normal or common.
   b. Board games and chatting round the kitchen table.

page 21

1. If they didn't have the latest designer clothes, some children might feel they were the odd one out.

page 23

1. a. Dogs are friendly, loyal pets. **Opinion**
   b. It usually snows in the Alps in winter. **Fact**
   c. The Earth orbits the Sun whilst it spins on its axis. **Fact**
   d. The best show on the TV is *The Simpsons*. **Opinion**

page 25

1. It was funny because robbers wouldn't normally say 'thank you' to someone they had just robbed.
2. The manager says that the sports complex had 'stepped up security dramatically in recent months'.
3. The fact that they had practised so hard and for so long.

Practice Questions

page 27

1. Accept 2 examples from: radiators grin; headlights stare; shop doorways keep their mouths shut. **(2 marks)**
2. In the stage directions, which are usually in brackets. **(1 mark)**
3. Answers will vary. Examples:
   a. My little sister is as chatty as a parrot. **(1 mark)**
   b. The wind howled like a banshee. **(1 mark)**
   c. The branches hung low like spindly fingers. **(1 mark)**
   d. My hair stood on end like a toilet brush. **(1 mark)**
4.

	Fiction	Non-fiction
sci-fi story	✓	
autobiography		✓
explanation		✓
poem	✓	

(4 marks)

5 Dear Sir/Madam

I rarely complain about anything but after the shocking meal I had when ~~I was in your restaurant last night~~ I feel compelled to put pen to paper.

The pasta was barely warm and extremely soggy. This is an easy product to cook so it's not difficult to get it right . The waiter, in a sulk about something, ~~brought our drinks~~ after a very long wait. I was on the verge of drinking the water from the vase of flowers in front of me. In this day and age, when ~~unemployment is at an all-time high~~, I would have thought he would want to do his best! **(11 marks)**

FICTION WRITING

Test Yourself Questions
page 29
1 Answers will vary. Example:

As we inched towards the cliff edge, we saw a boat with billowing white sails gliding across the horizon. From the bow, braving the wild weather, a silhouette gestured to us to come aboard.

page 31
1 Answers may vary. Examples:

asking a question; dialogue; starting in the middle of the action.

page 33
1 A haiku usually describes something to do with nature. It has three lines: five syllables in first line, seven in the second line, five in the third line.

2 A limerick has five lines.

3 A concrete poem takes the shape of whatever it is about.

Practice Questions
page 35
1 Answers will vary. Accept appropriate descriptive paragraphs describing the action and dilemma as the two characters find themselves trapped. Look for a range of sentence starters, figurative language and exciting adjectives. **(5 marks)**

2 Answers will vary. A haiku should have five syllables in the first line, seven in the second and five in the third (last) line. A concrete poem takes the shape of its subject. **(5 marks)**

NON-FICTION WRITING
Test Yourself Questions
page 37
1 bold title; subheadings; bold/coloured fonts and underlining; bullet points; pictures or diagrams; contents page, an index and a glossary in books

page 39
1 emotive language; repetition; rhetorical questions; statistics to back up your point; flattery; exaggeration

page 41
1 **a.** A visit to an art gallery – **a recount / chronological report**.

b. Nocturnal animals – **non-chronological report / information text**.

2 Answers will vary. Accept suitable timeline.

page 43
1 Accept any five from the following:
headline; by-line; lead paragraph; who, what, where, when, why, how; main body; sources; eyewitnesses; direct quotes; pictures and captions; summary

page 45
1 Answers may vary. Examples:

a. The Head Teacher will surely give us a snow day!

b. It's at least one metre deep and my mum's car is broken.

c. OK, let's see what happens but I'm not going in.

d. I'm not either but I expect Tommo's mum makes him go!

Practice Questions
page 47
1 Answers will vary. Appropriate features of an information leaflet should be included and cover the subheadings asked for. **(18 marks)**

2 A source might be an eyewitness to the events being reported or someone who has been given information/ heard information about the events. Source quotes can be direct speech. **(1 mark)**

3 emotive language; repetition; rhetorical questions; statistics to back up your point; flattery; exaggeration **(6 marks)**

4 Accept any four from the following:
rhetorical questions; catch phrase or slogan; bold and colourful font; images; special offer; imperative verbs; celebrity endorsement **(4 marks)**

GRAMMAR AND PUNCTUATION
Test Yourself Questions
page 49
1 it – the distance; them – Fred and Aisha

2 That bike isn't yours! It's mine!

page 51
1 Erin wriggled through the gap (adverbial) and in a matter of minutes (adverbial) was free.

2 Once the electric fence had been activated, even the most desperate animals couldn't escape.

page 53

1 a. (I was drinking) my juice when the phone rang.
   b. Just then the car (crashed) into the brick wall.
   c. I (eat) my supper every evening before I (watch) television.
   d. I didn't think I (could) climb the mountain but I did!
   e. After I (had practised) my spellings all week, I scored top marks in my test.

page 55

1 Some children were heading towards the beach when an adult came towards them waving a flag. It was the coastguard. He told them the weather had changed and they couldn't go in the sea. The children picked up their clothes and turned back to the path.

2 I went to my room and in it was the biggest mess imaginable! After I had cleared it, I went to the kitchen and sat at the table.

page 57

1 A main clause makes sense on its own. A subordinate clause cannot stand alone / does not make sense on its own.

2 Answers will vary. Examples:
   and; but; or; because; although; if; so; when

3 Answers will vary. Example:
   I like bread **but** I don't like toast; You won't be allowed to play out **unless** you do your homework.

page 59

1 Answers will vary. Examples:
   a. What do horses eat?
   b. Where is Australia?
   c. What time do you go to bed?

page 61

1 a. "There really isn't much point in packing a picnic," said Joe.
   b. "Well, it's not going to rain forever," Brogan pointed out. "Look over there – I can see a patch of blue sky."
   c. "Good for you," said Joe grumpily. "Do you really think the sun will come out though?"

page 63

1 a. The children were swiftly rescued – **passive**.
   b. The older children pulled the youngest to safety first – **active**.
   c. Everyone climbed onto the bus. – **active**
   d. Some children were driven home by their parents. – **passive**

page 65

1 Accept appropriate choice of parentheses and subordinate clauses in context; b. has to be brackets. Examples:
   a. I couldn't be bothered to go swimming – I was feeling a bit under the weather – so I stayed at home.
   b. We were amazed by the trapeze artists at the circus (they were a big improvement on last year's).
   c. Having been there on holiday before, a couple of times in fact, we knew our way around.
   d. Houdini, the famous escapologist, featured on a TV documentary last night.

page 67

1 Jake's mum's chicken pie wasn't the best. She'd burnt its edges as she'd left it in the oven too long. They should've gone out to Charlie's Chippy, thought Jake.

Practice Questions

page 69

1

Proper nouns	Common nouns	
	Nouns we can see or touch	Nouns we can't see or touch
Antarctica	flock	strength
Prince George	hand	despair
July	flower	fear
Jupiter	dog	bravery
United Kingdom	house	pity

(3 marks: award only 2 marks for 10–14 correctly placed nouns and only 1 mark for 7–9)

2 I ate my dinner quickly **or** I was eating my dinner quickly.   **(1 mark)**

3 a. My mother couldn't finish the horror story.   **(1 mark)**
   b. The heating has been on so the house must be warm now.   **(1 mark)**
   c. Would it be possible to leave the theatre now?   **(1 mark)**

4 Answers will vary. The sentence should include a main clause which makes sense on its own and a subordinate clause introduced by a conjunction such as because, although, even though... and so on. Example:
   We decided to walk the dog, even though it was getting close to bedtime.   **(1 mark)**

5 We had salad <u>and</u> bread for tea <u>but</u> nothing at bedtime. The next morning we were tired <u>and</u> hungry. There was some cereal on the table <u>yet</u> no sign of any milk. **(2 marks)**

6 Charlotte hurt her finger at the park and <u>she</u> had to have <u>it</u> bandaged. The nurse praised <u>her</u> for being brave and <u>she</u> gave <u>her</u> a special plaster.

(2 marks: award only 1 mark for 4 pronouns correctly underlined)

7 <u>Soon</u> Harry reached the cellar where he stumbled <u>awkwardly</u> over a <u>carelessly</u> discarded pizza box. Trying not to make a sound, Harry crept <u>with great caution</u> into the gloom… **(2 marks: award only 1 mark for 3–4 correctly identified)**

SPELLING

Test Yourself Questions

page 71

1 a. sister liberi – **irresistible**
   b. little aire – **illiterate**
   c. rail ration – **irrational**
   d. glaci olli – **illogical**

page 73

1 a. residential
   b. facial
   c. financial
   d. influential

page 75

1 a. The passenger (preferred)(transferring) her suitcase using the (unwieldy) trolley.
   b. I kept (receiving) letters with a (weird) stamp advertising (abseiling) events.

page 77

1 a. The new Head Teacher was soon **accepted** by the staff.
   b. The new Head Teacher had an amazing **effect** on the children.

Practice Questions

page 79

1

happy	**un**happy
understand	**mis**understand
appropriate	**in**appropriate
polite	**im**polite

(4 marks)

2 a. We <u>eight</u> our <u>pairs</u> and went out to play.
       ate   pears **(1 mark)**
   b. <u>They're</u> <u>hare</u> has been cut very short.
       Their   hair **(1 mark)**

3

influence	influential
division	divisible
horror	horrible
present	presentable

(4 marks)

4 We have only <u>brought</u> our <u>rough</u> sketches, <u>although</u> if we have <u>enough</u> time we <u>ought</u> to be able to complete them. **(2 marks)**

5 a. scene **(1 mark)**
   b. dessert **(1 mark)**

6 a. Some cracks have appeared in my (<u>ceiling</u>/ cieling).
   b. My parents (recieved/<u>received</u>) my school report last night.
   c. The Latin expression *carpe diem* means '(<u>seize</u>/ sieze) the day'. **(3 marks)**

SPEAKING AND LISTENING

Test Yourself Questions

page 81

1 A monotone voice is a voice with no expression and one tone throughout.

2 Body language can be used to emphasise points the speaker feels very strongly about, for example by gesticulating (gestures), clenching hands or banging fists.

3 Pictures and/or props; use of ICT (e.g. Powerpoint).

page 83

1 Closed questions don't give any scope for a detailed answer. The answer might be a one-word answer such as yes or no.

2 Hot-seating is when someone takes on the role of someone you would like to interview.

3 Answers will vary. Example:
Drama enables you to gain confidence in performing to an audience.

Practice Questions

page 85

1 Answers will vary. Questions should be open and relevant to Nelson Mandela. **(6 marks)**

2 Answers will vary. Accept appropriate speech supporting healthy eating. **(6 marks)**

SATs PRACTICE QUESTIONS

1 a. Mobile phones emit radiation which could be harmful. **(1 mark)**
   b. Constantly. **(1 mark)**
   c. You could phone emergency services or contact someone quickly from wherever you are. **(1 mark)**

2 a.

- a piano — in the bar
- wood panelling — through the window
- fine views — in the compartments
- finest crystal glasses — in the dining car

(2 marks: 2 marks for all 4 correct, 1 mark for 2)

b. The word 'snakes' is used to describe the train's journey across Europe because the train doesn't travel in a straight line; it moves like a snake, curving smoothly round mountains and over rivers.

(1 mark)

c. Personal steward **(1 mark)**

3 a. Death **(1 mark)**

b. Personification of the wind shows how much pain the climber is in: the wind 'cut' into his face, 'blasting' his lips numb and 'caking' his eyelashes with thick frost.

(1 mark)

c. The climber has felt the rope vibrate and shake, which makes him think he's going to fall into the crevasse. **(1 mark)**

d. A type of clip to attach the climber to a rope. **(1 mark)**

4 These books are **his**.
This dog is **theirs**.
That car is **ours**. **(1 mark)**

5 The farm dog rounded up all the sheep. ☑ **(1 mark)**

6

Noun	Adjective
group	dedicated
walk	brisk

(1 mark)

7 Accept insertion of an appropriate adverb, spelt correctly, e.g.: cautiously, carefully, slowly, quickly. **(1 mark)**

8 a. The cat fell asleep in front of the crackling fire. **(1 mark)**

b. The man fired a pistol to start the cross-country race. **(1 mark)**

9 The children stood before **the** castle. There was **an** ancient gate with huge hinges. With **a** mighty heave, they pushed it open.

(1 mark)

10 Hassan went to the doctor (because) he had a sore throat (and) a temperature. **(1 mark)**

11 We were taken on the bus to the seaside by Mum and Dad.
We were shown around by the lady who owned the hotel. **(1 mark)**

12 Joseph quickly finished (his homework.)

(1 mark)

13 "We haven't got all day," Brogan said impatiently. "Hurry up!" **(1 mark)**

14 <u>As we were driving to school</u>, we noticed that someone had fallen on the footpath.
<u>When we arrived at the swimming pool</u>, the attendants told us it was closed.
The park, <u>which had been closed for improvements</u>, reopened at the weekend.

(1 mark)

15 As he walked towards the church**,** Tom was aware of someone following him. **(1 mark)**

Abbreviations – Shortened word forms

Active voice – The subject of the sentence is doing or being; the object is having it done to them/it

Adjective – A word that describes a noun

Adverb – A word that tells us more about a verb (how, where, when), an adjective, another adverb or a whole clause

Adverbial – A word, phrase or clause that tells us more about a verb (how, where, when)

Alliteration – Repetition of the initial letters of words next to or close to each other

Annotated – Labelled

Apostrophe – A punctuation mark used to show omission (contraction) or possession

Assonance – Repetition of vowel sounds inside words

Bias – Supporting one point of view over another

Blurb – A brief overview of a book

Body language – Using your body to get your point across or to get the audience's attention

Brackets – Can show parenthesis

By-line – Tells the reader the name of the person who has written the report

Caption – Brief description of what is shown in a picture

Chronological – In the order that something happens

Cohesion – When your whole piece of writing fits together clearly so that it makes sense

Colloquialisms – Expressions in informal, everyday language

Command – Gives an instruction

Command verb – A verb used to give a command or instruction

Commas – Can show parenthesis

Common nouns – Nouns for people, animals and objects

Comprehension – Understanding

Conjunction – Links two words, phrases or clauses

Contraction – A word that has been made shorter

Coordinating conjunction – Links two words, phrases or clauses of equal importance

Dashes – Can show parenthesis

Determiner – A word that introduces a noun such as 'the', 'a', 'some' and 'those'

Direct speech – A sentence in inverted commas showing the exact words spoken by someone

Emotive language – Emotional language used to express feelings

Empathise – To understand and share the feelings of someone else

Emphasis – Stress

Etymology – The origin of words

Exclamation – A sentence that shows feelings like fear, anger, happiness or excitement

Expanded noun phrase – A phrase with a noun as its main word with other words that tell us more about that noun

Fact – A piece of information that is true

Fiction – Made-up stories

Figurative language – The descriptive language used to create imagery

Formal speech – Speaking and writing using correct grammar and vocabulary

Fronted adverbial – An adverb or adverbial coming at the start of a sentence

Genre – Type or kind of writing

Gesticulate – To use gestures to emphasise your point

Homophones – Words that sound the same but have different spellings and different meanings

Hook – It's what grabs the reader's attention (think of a fish grabbing onto a hook on a fishing line)

Imagery – The use of figurative language to help the reader visualise what is being described

Infer – To form an opinion about something based on the information given rather than from an explicit statement

Informal speech – Relaxed, chatty way of speaking and writing used with family and friends

Inverted commas – The punctuation at the start and end of direct speech

Jingle – A short verse or tune designed to be memorable

Main clause – A clause that can make sense as a sentence

Metaphor – When the writer says the object that is being compared actually is the thing it's compared to

Modal verbs – Verbs that show possibility or likelihood

Monotone – Using no expression, so your voice has only one tone

Non-chronological – Not in the order that something happens

Non-fiction – Factual information

Noun phrase – A phrase where a noun is the main word

Nouns – Naming words for people, places, animals and things

Omission – Leaving a letter or letters out

Onomatopoeia – Words that sound like the thing they are describing

Opinion – What you personally think about something

Parentheses – The punctuation marks used to indicate parenthesis

Parenthesis – A word or phrase inserted into a sentence as an explanation or afterthought

Passive voice – When the subject isn't carrying out the action but is being acted upon by someone or something

Past – A verb tense showing what has happened

Past perfect – A verb tense formed from the past tense of the verb 'have' + the past participle of the main verb

Past progressive – A verb tense showing a continuous action in the past

Glossary

Personification – Giving human characteristics to a non-human thing

Possession – Ownership

Possessive determiner – A determiner showing ownership of the noun that immediately follows

Possessive pronoun – A word to show ownership

Prefix – A string of letters added to the start of a word to change its meaning

Preposition – Shows the relationship between the noun or pronoun and other words in the clause or sentence

Present – A verb tense showing what is happening now

Present perfect – A verb tense formed from the present tense of the verb 'have' + the past participle of the main verb

Present progressive – A verb tense showing a continuous action in the present

Pronoun – A word that replaces a noun

Proofreading – Checking your writing for errors and ways to improve it

Proper nouns – Nouns that name particular things. They begin with a capital letter

Pun – A type of word play where the word can have more than one meaning

Question – A sentence that asks something

Quote – Direct speech by a source or witness

Recount – Report retelling an event that has happened

Relative clause – A subordinate clause introduced by a relative pronoun

Relative pronoun – The words 'who', 'which', 'that' and 'whose' which introduce a relative clause

Rhetorical question – A question used for effect and with no answer expected

Root word – A word in its own right, without a prefix or a suffix

Scan – A quick reading technique to help you find specific words, phrases and clauses in a text

Silent letter – A letter that was once pronounced but now isn't

Simile – A comparison of two things with similar characteristics, using the words 'like' or 'as'

Skim read – A quick reading technique to help you get the gist (the main idea) of a text

Slang – Very informal language used when speaking to friends

Slogan – A short, memorable phrase in an advert

Source – Someone who gives a journalist information about the events being reported

Standard English – Using the rules of English grammar correctly

Statement – A sentence that gives information

Stress – When you either increase the vowel length or loudness of the syllable or both

Subordinate clause – A clause which depends on the main clause to make sense

Subordinating conjunction – A conjunction that introduces a subordinate clause

Suffix – A letter or a string of letters added to the root word to change or add to its meaning

Syllable – A single, unbroken sound containing at least one vowel

Synopsis/précis – Brief summary

Verb – A word for an action or state of being

Index